Insights You Need from
Harvard
Business
Review

THE YEAR
IN TECH 2022

Insights You Need from Harvard Business Review

Business is changing. Will you adapt or be left behind?

Get up to speed and deepen your understanding of the topics that are shaping your company's future with the **Insights You Need from Harvard Business Review** series. Featuring HBR's smartest thinking on fast-moving issues—blockchain, cybersecurity, AI, and more—each book provides the foundational introduction and practical case studies your organization needs to compete today and collects the best research, interviews, and analysis to get it ready for tomorrow.

You can't afford to ignore how these issues will transform the landscape of business and society. The Insights You Need series will help you grasp these critical ideas—and prepare you and your company for the future.

Books in the series include:

Agile

Artificial Intelligence

Blockchain

Climate Change

Coronavirus: Leadership and Recovery

Customer Data and Privacy

Cybersecurity

Global Recession

Monopolies and Tech Giants

Racial Justice

Strategic Analytics

The Year in Tech 2021

The Year in Tech 2022

Insights You Need from
**Harvard
Business
Review**

THE YEAR
IN TECH 2022

Harvard Business Review Press
Boston, Massachusetts

Copyright 2021 Harvard Business School Publishing Corporation
All rights reserved
Printed in the United States of America

10 9 8 7 6 5 4 3 2 1

No part of this publication may be reproduced, stored in or introduced into a retrieval system, or transmitted, in any form, or by any means (electronic, mechanical, photocopying, recording, or otherwise), without the prior permission of the publisher. Requests for permission should be directed to permissions@harvardbusiness.org, or mailed to Permissions, Harvard Business School Publishing, 60 Harvard Way, Boston, Massachusetts 02163.

The web addresses referenced in this book were live and correct at the time of the book's publication but may be subject to change.

Library of Congress Cataloging-in-Publication Data

Names: Harvard Business Review Press.
Title: The year in tech, 2022 : the insights you need from Harvard Business Review.
Other titles: Insights you need from Harvard Business Review.
Description: Boston, Massachusetts : Harvard Business Review Press, [2022] | Series: Insights you need from Harvard Business Review | Includes index.
Identifiers: LCCN 2021022444 | ISBN 9781647821753 (paperback) | ISBN 9781647821760 (ebook)
Subjects: LCSH: Business—Technological innovations. | Industrial management. | Success in business.
Classification: LCC HD45 .Y68 2022 | DDC 658.5/14—dc23
LC record available at https://lccn.loc.gov/2021022444

ISBN: 978-1-64782-175-3
eISBN: 978-1-64782-176-0

The paper used in this publication meets the requirements of the American National Standard for Permanence of Paper for Publications and Documents in Libraries and Archives Z39.48-1992.

Contents

Introduction

Business Reality Is Rapidly Closing In on Science Fiction　　　xi

Disruptions are coming faster than expected

by Larry Downes

Section 1

Managing New Essential Tech

1. **A Practical Guide to Building Ethical AI**　　　3

   AI doesn't just scale solutions—it also scales risk.

   by Reid Blackman

2. **How Companies Are Using Virtual Reality to Develop**　　　17
   Employees' Soft Skills

   *VR enables immersive, interactive learning
   experiences.*

   by Jeanne C. Meister

Contents

3. **Want to See the Future of Digital Health Tools?**   27
   Look to Germany.

   "Prescribable applications" could transform health care.

   by Ariel D. Stern, Henrik Matthies, Julia Hagen,
   Jan B. Brönneke, and Jörg F. Debatin

4. **Building a Transparent Supply Chain**   35

   Blockchain can enhance trust, efficiency, and speed.

   by Vishal Gaur and Abhinav Gaiha

Section 2

Looking Ahead to Future Tech

5. **What Brain-Computer Interfaces Could Mean**   61
   for the Future of Work

   Imagine preparing your next presentation using only your thoughts.

   by Alexandre Gonfalonieri

6. **Get Ready for the Quantum Computing Revolution**   71

   Unhackable encryption could be on the horizon.

   by Shohini Ghose

7. **The Commercial Space Age Is Here**   81

   Private space travel is just the beginning.

   by Matt Weinzierl and Mehak Sarang

Section 3

Upgrading the Tech Industry

8. **What's Next for Silicon Valley?**   97

   The era of the tech titans may be nearing an end.

   by Maëlle Gavet

9. **What It's Like to Be a Black Man in Tech**   109

   You're constantly wondering, "How long can I last?"

   by LeRon L. Barton

10. **Social Media Companies Should Self-Regulate. Now.** 121

    *Lessons from industries that have done
    so successfully.*

    by Michael A. Cusumano, Annabelle Gawer, and David B. Yoffie

11. **How Green Is Your Software?**   131

    *Beware digital technologies that worsen
    environmental problems.*

    by Sanjay Podder, Adam Burden, Shalabh Kumar Singh,

    and Regina Maruca

About the Contributors   143

Index   149

Introduction

BUSINESS REALITY IS RAPIDLY CLOSING IN ON SCIENCE FICTION

by Larry Downes

As organizations worldwide shake off the impact of compound crises, new and emerging technologies shine brightly as a rare source of optimism, with the potential to jump-start renewed growth and even improve the human condition. This book explores a remarkable range of new and future business innovations, using technologies as varied as artificial intelligence, virtual reality, brain-computer interfaces, and quantum computing. One piece even proclaims the dawn of the commercial space age.

What's most striking about these visions is how today's business reality is closing in on what was once futuristic science fiction. As HR consultant Jeanne C. Meister points out, virtual reality technology—a distant dream only a few years ago—is already being employed to resolve a "soft skills" crisis. Businesses are now using VR to help their people develop their abilities in customer service, presentations, and employee evaluations. Another piece shows how digital health care, including the telehealth and remote diagnostic approaches that became familiar during the Covid-19 pandemic, can be more effective and equitable than yesterday's broken system. And a third examines how blockchain technology is being deployed to improve the safety and efficiency of disparate supply chains for a variety of critical manufacturing applications.

Many of these advances will inevitably come as shocks to existing industries. They will arrive sooner than expected and change business practices in unpredictable ways. Many will come from surprising sources, including new entrants to mature markets. As author David Weinberger pointed out in last year's edition of *The Year in Tech*, the internet has "disrupted not only our old ways of doing things, but even our idea of how progress works."

"Disruption" remains the operative word this year. Indeed, some of the applications described in these pages will likely turn out to be what Paul Nunes and I have termed "Big Bang Disruptions"—innovations built on technologies that are both better and cheaper than existing offerings. That powerful one-two punch guarantees rapid and chaotic reconfigurations of industries, some of which may not have experienced significant change in several generations of managers.

The chaos of Big Bang Disruption challenges the management abilities and institutional resilience of all business as they struggle for pole position in the emerging ecosystems that new technologies create. Yet, at the same time, these disruptions often produce better quality and better prices for consumers.

This paradox is not new. Whether the most disruptive technologies are viewed as helpful or harmful frequently depends on who is using them. Indeed, as even the occasional consumer of science fiction knows, visions of the future often neatly divide themselves between utopia and dystopia. The *Star Trek* franchise, for one, contrasts the dream of a tech-enabled Federation against the nightmare of the tech-dependent Borg. The former uses technology to maximize diversity and individual potential among a galaxy-spanning alliance of planets; the latter seeks to eradicate every trace of individual thought and will through violent conquest and forced technological "assimilation."

Such conflicts resonate strongly with us because technology is the defining feature of modern civilization. It reflects and amplifies the best—and the worst—of human development. But this isn't just compelling drama. *Star Trek*'s creators asked us to acknowledge the elements of both visions that are present in the world we already live in, inviting us to do what we can to improve the balance.

Likewise, the articles in this collection balance their authors' justified enthusiasm for exciting developments in technology with anxiety about its potential for abuse. Indeed, the single common thread that ties together all of the new and future applications they describe is *risk*. AI consultant Alexandre Gonfalonieri, for example, explains how brain-computer interfaces may help employers monitor the stress and fatigue of employees operating dangerous equipment in real time. Preventing accidents before they happen is, of course, a utopian goal. But the ethical dangers of such intimate data collection are obvious.

Similarly, machine-learning algorithms and other applications of AI may free us from the most tedious decision-making tasks. But as business and tech ethicist Reid Blackman points out, that liberation comes at the risk of repeating and amplifying existing racial, gender, and economic biases—human failings that are today epidemic in the tech sector itself, as author LeRon L. Barton describes in deeply personal terms.

The focus on risk in each of these articles is both striking and appropriate. As technology has become more entwined with our daily lives, it's not surprising that concerns over potential misuse and abuse have grown. When digital technology was limited to back-office systems and consumer electronics, it was easy to celebrate and embrace it without reservation. The innovations described in this collection have the potential to go much further, revolutionizing business and even our personal lives.

The rewards may be great, but so too are the risks, and for better and for worse, we've lost our innocence about them. Since 2018, trust in the tech sector overall has fallen precipitously, especially in the United States. This despite the vital role tech played in health care, education, remote working, and delivery of essential goods in keeping the world running during the Covid-19 pandemic.

Technology has also come increasingly under the microscope of governments. The authors ask some big questions here: Can regulators assess and mitigate the risks of new algorithms? Can courts and legislatures redefine antitrust for a networked economy? Will governments willingly let go of their monopoly on space travel?

Here the forecast is cloudy, with a strong chance of damaging storms. Throughout history, and especially over the last decade, regulators have a poor track record of correcting, let alone forestalling, the unintended

FIGURE I-1

Technology sector trust decline deepens

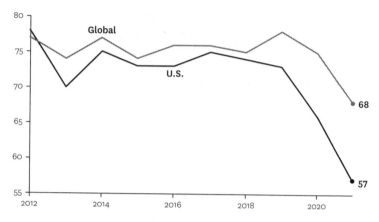

Source: Data: Edelman Trust Barometer; chart: Axios Visuals, https://autos.yahoo.com /exclusive-trust-tech-cratered-over-100326969.html.

economic, environmental, and social side effects that accompany disruptive leaps in technology.

The main problem with regulating the tech sector is the speed of change. Technology, as we are reminded on a daily basis, improves at an accelerating pace, while governments, at best, remain incremental, deliberative, and, sadly, often paralyzed by partisanship, bureaucracy, and special interests. When lawmakers finally act, many times it's too late to solve the problem they initially identified. Worse, their partial fixes may create even more-serious problems.

Business leaders in particular, as professors Michael A. Cusumano, Annabelle Gawer, and David B. Yoffie argue persuasively, have a crucial role to play in mediating and moderating the worst excesses of both unfettered innovation and legislative missteps. To do so, they must take responsibility for regulating themselves. They must act conscientiously in deploying new applications of technology, warding off as many negative consequences as possible. They must not leave the duty of addressing issues of security, user autonomy, equity, and competition solely to engineers. And they must be actively engaged in dialogue with governments at all levels to ensure that cures for true market failures caused by fast-moving technologies do not prove worse than the diseases they target.

The authors of the articles that follow share, each in their own individual way, an optimism that the future we experience will be significantly better thanks to the technologies they describe. Rather than ignoring the accompanying risks, each piece offers concrete recommendations for how best to deploy these new innovations and how best to control them. They offer a balance, with techniques for minimizing costs and maximizing benefits.

This brings us back to fast-approaching science fiction. To thrive in the technological now, let alone the fast-approaching future, we must all commit to working toward the utopia of the Federation, and to resisting the dystopian temptations of the Borg. We can do it. But we'd better hurry. The future will be here any minute.

Section 1

MANAGING NEW ESSENTIAL TECH

1

A PRACTICAL GUIDE TO BUILDING ETHICAL AI

by Reid Blackman

Companies are leveraging data and artificial intelligence to create scalable solutions—but they're also scaling their reputational, regulatory, and legal risks. For instance, Los Angeles is suing IBM for allegedly misappropriating data it collected with its ubiquitous weather app. Optum is being investigated by regulators for creating an algorithm that allegedly recommended that doctors and nurses pay more attention to white patients than to sicker Black patients. Goldman Sachs is being investigated by regulators for using an AI algorithm that allegedly discriminated against women by granting larger credit limits to men than women on their Apple Cards. Facebook infamously granted Cambridge Analytica, a political firm, access to the personal data of more than 50 million users.

Just a few years ago, discussions of "data ethics" and "AI ethics" were reserved for nonprofit organizations and academics. Today, the biggest tech companies in the world—Microsoft, Facebook, Twitter, Google, and others—are putting together fast-growing teams to tackle the ethical problems that arise from the widespread collection, analysis, and use of massive troves of data, particularly when that data is used to train machine-learning models, also known as AI.

These companies are investing in answers to once esoteric ethical questions because they've realized one simple truth: Failing to operationalize data and AI ethics is a threat to the bottom line. Missing the mark can expose companies to reputational, regulatory, and legal risks, but that's not the half of it. Failing to operationalize data and AI ethics leads to wasted resources, inefficiencies in product development and deployment, and even an inability to use data to train AI models at all. For example, Amazon engineers reportedly spent years working on AI hiring software but eventually scrapped the program because they couldn't figure out how to create a model that doesn't systematically discriminate against women. Sidewalk Labs, a subsidiary of Google, faced massive backlash by citizens and local government officials over their plans to build an IoT-fueled "smart city" within Toronto, due to a lack of clear ethical standards for the project's data handling. The company ultimately terminated the project at a loss of two years of work and US$50 million.

Despite the costs of getting it wrong, most companies grapple with data and AI ethics through ad hoc discussions on a per-product basis. With no clear protocol in place on how to identify, evaluate, and mitigate the risks, teams end up either overlooking risks, scrambling to solve issues as they come up, or crossing their fingers in the hope that the problem will resolve itself. When companies have attempted to tackle the issue at scale, they've tended to implement strict, imprecise, and overly broad policies that lead to false positives in risk identification and stymied production. These problems grow by orders of magnitude when you introduce third-party vendors, who may or may not be thinking about these questions at all.

Companies need a plan for mitigating risk—how to use data and develop AI products without falling into ethical pitfalls along the way. Just like other risk-management strategies, an operationalized approach to data and AI ethics must systematically and exhaustively identify ethical risks throughout the organization, from IT to HR to marketing to product and beyond.

What Not to Do

Putting the larger tech companies to the side, there are three standard approaches to data and AI ethical risk mitigation, none of which bear fruit.

First, there is the *academic approach*. Academics—and I speak from 15 years of experience as a former professor of philosophy—are fantastic at rigorous and systematic inquiry. Those academics who are ethicists (typically found in philosophy departments) are adept at spotting ethical problems, their sources, and how to think through them. But while academic ethicists might seem like a perfect match, given the need for systematic identification and mitigation of ethical risks, they unfortunately tend to ask different questions than businesses. For the most part, academics ask, "Should we do this? Would it be good for society overall? Does it conduce to human flourishing?" Businesses, on the other hand, tend to ask, "Given that we are going to do this, how can we do it without making ourselves vulnerable to ethical risks?"

The result is academic treatments that do not speak to the highly particular, concrete uses of data and AI. This translates to the absence of clear directives to the developers on the ground and the senior leaders who need to identify and choose among a set of risk-mitigation strategies.

Next is the *"on the ground" approach.* Within businesses those asking the questions are standardly enthusiastic engineers, data scientists, and product managers. They know to ask the business-relevant risk-related questions precisely because they are the ones making the products to achieve particular business goals. What they lack, however, is the kind of training that academics receive. As a result, they do not have the skill, knowledge, and experience to answer ethical questions systematically, exhaustively, and efficiently. They also lack a critical ingredient: institutional support.

Finally, there are companies (not to mention countries) rolling out *high-level AI ethics principles.* Google and Microsoft, for instance, trumpeted their principles years ago. The difficulty comes in operationalizing those principles. What, exactly, does it mean to be "for fairness?" What are engineers to do when confronted with the dozens of definitions and accompanying metrics for fairness in the computer science literature? Which metric is the right one in any given case, and who makes that judgment? For most companies—including those tech companies who are actively trying to solve the problem—there are no clear answers to these questions. Indeed, seeming coalescence around a shared set of abstract values actually obscures widespread misalignment.

How to Operationalize Data and AI Ethics

AI ethics does not come in a box. Given the varying values of companies across dozens of industries, a data and AI ethics program must be tailored to the specific business and regulatory needs that are relevant to the company. However, here are seven steps toward building a customized, operationalized, scalable, and sustainable data and AI ethics program.

1. Identify existing infrastructure that a data and AI ethics program can leverage. The key to a successful creation of a data and AI ethics program is using the power and authority of existing infrastructure, such as a data governance board that convenes to discuss privacy, cyber, compliance, and other data-related risks. This allows concerns from those "on the ground" (e.g., product owners and managers) to bubble up and, when necessary, they can in turn elevate key concerns to relevant executives. Governance board buy-in works for a few reasons:

1. The executive level sets the tone for how seriously employees will take these issues.

2. A data and AI ethics strategy needs to dovetail with the general data and AI strategy, which is devised at the executive level.

3. Protecting the brand from reputational, regulatory, and legal risk is ultimately a C-suite responsibility, and they need to be alerted when high-stakes issues arise.

If such a body does not exist, then companies can create one—an ethics council or committee, for example—with ethics-adjacent personnel, such as those in cyber, risk and compliance, privacy, and analytics. It may also be advisable to include external subject matter experts, including ethicists.

2. Create a data and AI ethical risk framework that is tailored to your industry. A good framework comprises, at a minimum, an articulation of the ethical standards—including the ethical nightmares—of the company, an identification of the relevant external and internal stakeholders, a recommended governance structure, and an articulation of how that structure will be maintained in the face of changing personnel and circumstances. It is important to establish KPIs and a quality assurance program to measure the continued effectiveness of the tactics carrying out your strategy.

A robust framework also makes clear how ethical risk mitigation is built into operations. For instance, it should identify the ethical standards that data collectors, product developers, and product managers and owners must adhere to. It should also articulate a clear process by which ethical concerns are elevated to more-senior leadership or to an ethics committee. All companies should ask whether there are processes in place that vet for biased algorithms, privacy violations, and unexplainable outputs.

Still, frameworks also need to be tailored to a company's industry. In finance, it is important to think about how digital identities are determined and how international transactions can be ethically safe. In health care there will need to be extra protections built around privacy, particularly as AI enables the development of precision medicine. In the retail space, where recommendation engines loom large, it is important to develop methods to detect and mitigate associative bias, where recommendations flow from stereotypical and sometimes offensive associations with various populations.

3. Change how you think about ethics by taking cues from the successes in health care. Many senior leaders describe ethics in general—and data and AI ethics in particular—as "squishy" or "fuzzy," and argue it is not sufficiently "concrete" to be actionable. Leaders should take inspiration from health care, an industry that has been systematically focused on ethical risk mitigation since at least the 1970s. Key concerns about what constitutes privacy, self-determination, and informed consent, for example, have been explored deeply by medical ethicists, health-care practitioners, regulators, and lawyers. Those insights can be transferred to many ethical dilemmas around consumer data privacy and control.

For instance, companies attest to respect the users of their products, but what does that mean in practice? In health care, an essential requirement of demonstrating respect for patients is that they are treated only after granting their informed consent—understood to include consent that, at a minimum, does not result from lies, manipulation, or communications in words the patient cannot understand, such as impenetrable legalese or Latin medical terms. These same kinds of requirements can be brought to bear on how people's data is collected, used, and shared. Ensuring not only that users are informed of how their data is being used but also that they are informed early on and in a way that makes comprehension likely—for instance, by not burying the information in a long legal document—is one easy lesson to take from health care. The more general lesson is to break down big ethical concepts like privacy, bias, and "explainability" into infrastructures, processes, and practices that realize those values.

4. Optimize guidance and tools for product managers. While your framework provides high-level guidance, it's essential that guidance at the product level is granular. Take, for instance, the oft-lauded value of explainability in AI, a highly valued feature of machine-learning models that will likely be part of your framework. Standard machine-learning algorithms engage in pattern recognition too unwieldy for humans to grasp. But it is common—particularly when the outputs of the AI are potentially life-altering—to want or demand explanations for AI outputs. The problem is that there is often a tension between making outputs explainable, on the one hand, and making the outputs (e.g., predictions) accurate, on the other.

Product managers need to know how to make that trade-off, and customized tools should be developed to help product managers make those decisions. For example, companies can create a tool by which project managers can evaluate the importance of explainability for a given product. If explainability is desirable because it helps to ferret out bias in an algorithm, but biased outputs are not a concern for this particular machine-learning application, then that downgrades the importance of explainability relative to accuracy. If the outputs fall under regulations that require explanations—for instance, regulations in the banking industry that require banks to explain why someone has been turned down for a loan—then explainability will be imperative. The same goes for other relevant values, such as which, if any, of the dozens of metrics to use when determining whether a product delivers fair or equitable outputs.

5. Build organizational awareness. Ten years ago, corporations scarcely paid attention to cyber risks, but they certainly do now, and employees are expected to have a grasp of some of those risks. Anyone who touches data or AI products—be they in HR, marketing, or operations—should understand the company's data and AI ethics framework. Creating a culture in which a data and AI ethics strategy can be successfully deployed and maintained requires educating and upskilling employees, as well as empowering them to raise important questions at crucial junctures and raise key concerns to the appropriate deliberative body. Throughout this process, it's important to clearly articulate why data and AI ethics matters to the organization in a way that demonstrates that the commitment is not merely part of a public relations campaign.

6. Formally and informally incentivize employees to play a role in identifying AI ethical risks. As we've learned from numerous infamous examples, ethical standards are compromised when people are financially incentivized to act unethically. Similarly, failing to financially incentivize ethical actions can lead to them being deprioritized. A company's values are partly determined by how it directs financial resources. When employees don't see a budget behind scaling and maintaining a strong data and AI ethics program, they will turn their attention to what moves them forward in their career. Rewarding people for their efforts in promoting a data ethics program is essential.

7. Monitor impacts and engage stakeholders. Creating organizational awareness, ethics committees, and informed product managers, owners, engineers, and data collectors is all part of the development and, ideally, procurement process. But due to limited resources and time, and a general failure to imagine all the ways things can go wrong, it is important to monitor the impacts of the data and AI products that are on the market. A car can be built with airbags and crumple zones, but that doesn't mean it's safe to drive it at 100 mph down a side street. Similarly, AI products can be ethically developed but unethically deployed. There is both qualitative and quantitative research to be done here, particularly engaging stakeholders to determine how the product has affected them. Indeed, in the ideal scenario, relevant stakeholders are identified early in the development process and incorporated into an articulation of what the product does and does not do.

Operationalizing data and AI ethics is not an easy task. It requires buy-in from senior leadership and cross-functional collaboration. Companies that make the investment, however, will not only see mitigated risk but also more-efficient adoption of the technologies they need to forge ahead. And finally, they'll be exactly what their clients, consumers, and employees are looking for: trustworthy.

TAKEAWAYS

AI doesn't only scale solutions—it also scales ethical risk. To operationalize data and AI ethics, organizations should:

✓ Identify existing infrastructure that a data and AI ethics program can leverage.

✓ Create a risk framework that is tailored to their industry.

✓ Take cues from successes in health care.

✓ Optimize guidance and tools for product managers.

✓ Build organizational awareness.

✓ Incentivize employees to play a role in identifying AI ethical risks.

✓ Monitor impacts of AI products and engage stakeholders.

Adapted from content posted on hbr.org, October 15, 2020 (product #H05XNT).

2

HOW COMPANIES ARE USING VIRTUAL REALITY TO DEVELOP EMPLOYEES' SOFT SKILLS

by Jeanne C. Meister

Today's companies are facing a growing soft skills gap. Recent studies found that 59% of surveyed hiring managers and 89% of executives reported difficulty recruiting candidates with the requisite soft skills, such as communication, teamwork, and leadership.[1] And these soft skills are only becoming more essential (and more difficult to develop) with the growing prevalence of remote work. Without access to in-person training and education, what can businesses do to help their employees develop these vital skills?

One promising solution is virtual reality. Unlike traditional e-learning solutions, VR tools offer learners a truly immersive experience: These interactive programs can run on VR headsets—what most people likely think of when they hear "virtual reality"—or on standard mobile or desktop devices, and they allow employees to interact and role-play with avatars designed to mimic customers or other key stakeholders. According to Christopher Dede, a Harvard School of Education professor whose work focuses on applications of VR for education, "The future of VR is being immersed into an environment blending physical and digital worlds, where users interact via a headset, their computer, or their mobile device to role-play with an avatar or learn a new skill."

While traditional educational tools can sometimes feel boring or artificial, immersive VR training creates highly memorable, impactful experiences—without the potential risk of real-world consequences.

Not only can VR be highly effective, these tools can reduce both cost and logistical hurdles associated with traditional in-person training. Many employees already have access to mobile or desktop devices in their home offices, and VR programs are often more engaging and thus faster (and cheaper) to complete than alternative programs. A 2020 PwC study suggested that at scale, VR can be significantly more cost-effective than traditional soft skills training options, finding that employees completed VR programs up to four times faster than in-person trainings, and 1.5 times faster than e-learning programs—in large part because the immersive experience made it easier for learners to stay focused.[2] The study also found that employees who completed VR training felt almost four times more emotionally connected to the content than classroom learners did, and more than twice as connected as e-learners, illustrating the huge impact that VR can make.

To explore how leading companies are using VR for soft skills training today, my company (Future Workplace, an HR advisory firm) partnered with Mursion, a VR training platform, and a third-party independent research firm to survey more than 300 learning and development leaders across a variety of industries. Through our research, we found that more than two-thirds of respondents had either already implemented a VR training program for soft skills or planned to implement one within the next two years.[3]

In addition to looking at these quantitative adoption rates, we also conducted a qualitative analysis of how these programs are actually being used in practice. And while the survey revealed a whole spectrum of different applications for VR training, there were three common areas in which we found many companies had already begun leveraging VR to support soft skills development:

1. VR Simulations for Customer Service Training

First, VR simulations can provide a low-pressure way to practice high-stakes conversations. For example, one of the companies we surveyed was H&R Block, a global tax-preparation firm that onboards 5,000 new call center representatives every year, including 1,600 who join in the busy second half of the tax season. These entry-level employees are expected to field complex, emotionally charged calls from a variety of (often angry) customers within just a few days of starting at the company.

To succeed in this role, these employees need interpersonal skills such as active listening, calm under pressure, and the ability to summarize and resolve problems. As Kim Iorns, Director of Learning and Development for H&R Block, explained, "Fundamentally, our employees were doing all the things we wanted them to do, but there was something missing in our customer interactions. There was not enough of a human connection—so we made it a priority to focus our training on developing empathy."

To help their new hires develop these essential soft skills and ensure a consistently positive customer experience, H&R Block started using VR simulations in their onboarding process. Employees would use either a laptop or a VR headset to role-play a difficult customer conversation with a digital avatar, giving them an opportunity to practice these conversations and receive real-time feedback (without risking a real client relationship).

After implementing the VR training, H&R Block found that 70% of their customer service representatives preferred the new VR program to traditional learning tools and that the reps consistently reported that the VR simulations helped them improve their skills in handling difficult conversations. The company also saw a 50% decrease in dissatisfied customers, a 9.9% decrease in customer-handling times, and significantly faster issue-resolution times among the representatives who completed the program.

2. VR Simulations to Develop Presentation Skills

VR can also be an effective tool for improving presentation skills. For example, multinational technology and professional services provider Cognizant has been experimenting with leveraging VR simulations to train new hires to more clearly articulate their value proposition when pitching potential customers. These new hires are tasked with leveraging various kinds of data to explain a complex product and tell a compelling story—or risk losing important clients.

To help these employees hone their presentation skills, Cognizant developed a multistage VR-driven training program. First, the new hires complete an interactive digital course on data-driven storytelling. Next, they practice giving a client presentation with a VR avatar who role-plays as a customer. Finally, an AI engine built on Google NLP and ParallelDots API analyzes the presentation for key words, emotion, tone, and body language, and turns that analysis into actionable feedback for the user.

As Kshitij Nerurkar, North America Head of Cognizant's Learning Academy, explains, "Practicing client presentations is just one of VR's many soft skill applications, enabling new hires to practice presenting without needing to be in a classroom, and then receive instant feedback to fine-tune their communication and data-storytelling skills." This capacity for immediate feedback and essentially limitless rounds of practice (without relying on expensive, human training resources) is a key advantage of VR-powered learning tools.

3. VR Simulations for Employee Evaluation

Finally, VR can help managers evaluate employees' current skill levels for different key competencies, enabling them to more effectively allocate training resources and match skill profiles to job functions. For example, senior executives at HPE Financial Services (HPEFS) wanted to find a way to optimize training for their sales representatives—*before* the reps got in front of their valued, high-level customers. They decided to pilot a VR solution with 340 sales reps, in which the reps each conducted a 30-minute role-play exercise with an avatar designed to simulate a C-level customer. These role-plays were recorded and shared with the representatives' managers, who used them to determine whether the employee should be enrolled into further training at a basic, intermediate, or advanced level.

As Ronda Bowman, Global Learning & Development Leader for HPEFS, explained, "The VR for sales training was very helpful, as it enabled our reps to immerse themselves in a lifelike scenario and see how a customer might react to different sales techniques. For example, if a sales rep doesn't ask enough probing questions of the customer avatar, the avatar will stop engaging with the sales rep and start answering emails on her phone—just like a human would. Managers can then review the practice conversations and work with individual employees to identify areas for improvement, instead of waiting to hear negative feedback from real unhappy customers." The VR program not only provided HPEFS employees with improved training but also offered managers and HR teams improved visibility into their sales reps' current skills and opportunities for growth.

These are just a few of the ways our survey identified that VR can be used to narrow the soft skills gap. Especially as remote work becomes more common, it's likely that VR will become the desired platform for many soft skills training programs, from senior leadership development to new-hire onboarding. In fact, in my HBR article "21 HR Jobs of the Future," my coauthor and I propose an entirely new HR role dedicated to VR: a VR immersion counselor, focused on creating, facilitating, personalizing, and scaling the rollout of virtual reality for professional development. VR-powered education is poised to help the next generation of workers cultivate the essential soft skills they'll need to be valuable—and employable— in any organization.

TAKEAWAYS

Soft skills such as conflict resolution, teamwork, and leadership are more important than ever, but they can be difficult for employees to develop.

✓ Companies are using VR programs to support customer service training, presentation skills development, and employee evaluation. These applications may offer the opportunity to develop other soft skills as well.

✓ VR enables immersive experiences in which employees interact with an avatar to role-play difficult conversations and develop communication skills—without the risk of real-world consequences.

✓ Future uses of VR skills training might include senior leadership development and new-hire onboarding.

✓ With VR becoming the desired platform for many soft skills training programs, new HR roles may need to be created dedicated to VR professional development.

NOTES

1. Ryan Craig, "America's Skills Gap: Why It's Real, and Why It Matters," progressivepolicy.org, March 2019, https://www .progressivepolicy.org/wp-content/uploads/2019/03/SkillsGapFinal .pdf.

2. "The Effectiveness of Virtual Reality Soft Skills Training in the Enterprise: A Study," pwc.com, June 25, 2020, https://www.pwc .com/us/en/services/consulting/technology/emerging-technology /assets/pwc-understanding-the-effectiveness-of-soft-skills-training -in-the-enterprise-a-study.pdf.

3. *VR Changes the Game for Soft Skills Training*, Mursion and Future Workplace, December 2020, https://futureworkplace.com /vr-changes-the-game-for-soft-skills-training/.

Adapted from "How Companies Are Using VR to Develop Employees' Soft Skills," on hbr.org, January 11, 2021 (product #H0634C).

3

WANT TO SEE THE FUTURE OF DIGITAL HEALTH TOOLS? LOOK TO GERMANY.

by Ariel D. Stern, Henrik Matthies, Julia Hagen, Jan B. Brönneke, and Jörg F. Debatin

I n late 2019, Germany's parliament passed the Digital Healthcare Act (Digitale-Versorgung-Gesetz, or DVG)—an ambitious law designed to catalyze the digital transformation of the German health-care system, which has historically been a laggard in that area among peer countries. It is already leading to meaningful changes and will be a boon to the development and evaluation of digital health tools as well as the generation of insights into the value they create.

In the immediate wake of the DVG's passage, the Covid-19 pandemic has further underscored the need for safe and effective digital tools to support remote patient monitoring and care delivery worldwide. The timely introduction of the DVG means that Germany is poised to set an example for other countries in seeing what works (and what does not) in the adoption and diffusion of digital technologies for improving patient outcomes.

Perhaps the DVG's most important provisions are its formalization of "prescribable applications" (Digitale Gesundheitsanwendungen, or DiGA), which include standard software, software as a service (SaaS), and mobile as well as browser-based apps, and the creation of the Fast-Track Process, an accelerated regulatory path for companies to take their digital health applications to market. Following a streamlined review, an app can be added to a central registry of apps that can be prescribed by physicians and psychotherapists and will be reimbursed by all of Germany's statutory health insurance providers, which cover 90% of the population, or roughly 73 million individuals. The Fast-Track Process is run by the Federal Institute for Drugs and Medical Devices (Bundesinstitut für Arzneimittel und Medizinprodukte, or BfArM), which plays many of the same roles in Germany that the FDA does in the United States); BfArM also maintains the DiGA registry. The first five apps have already been added to the registry and offer support for patients to manage conditions including tinnitus, obesity, agoraphobia, osteoarthritis, and insomnia.

DVG promises to provide a standard care environment for manufacturers of new digital health tools to evaluate pricing strategies and understand how digital health applications fit into health-care practice and patients' everyday routines. The importance of such a major country mandating that all insurers have to pay for digital health apps is hard to overstate. (In the United States and other countries, it's still unclear to manufacturers of digital health products who will pay for their offerings.)

Entry to this market by digital health firms is, of course, not without legal and regulatory barriers. In order to be listed and remain in the DiGA registry and qualify for reimbursement by health insurers, an app must fulfill various requirements. These include data protection, information security, interoperability, and preliminary data on the benefits that the app provides. Furthermore, the app must already be CE-certified as a medical product in one of the EU's two lowest-risk classes (I or IIa).

If an app fulfills these requirements and provides evidence of its benefit ("positive care effects" associated with use), it can be listed directly. Otherwise, the app must demonstrate evidence of its benefits within 12 months of being added to the registry. This may be the demonstration of either a medical benefit (such as reduced duration of a disease) or patient-related improvements to the structure and process of the health-care system (such as an increase in patient adherence to a treatment program or improved health literacy). This incremental approach will prove especially valuable for smaller firms and startups, which frequently lack the funding to develop a certified medical product, deal with regulatory proceedings, and fund a large-scale scientific evaluation up front.

With at least 50 apps currently already in the Fast-Track Process and hundreds expected over the coming years from manufacturers worldwide, evaluation studies will create a wealth of data on how digital tools for remote patient care work in practice, which other payers and health systems can learn from. They will also be valuable in convincing health-care providers—for whom evidence is of paramount importance—of the value of digital tools, both generally and in particular use cases.

So what should health-care decision makers be looking out for? In addition to the evidence of digital health apps' benefits, it will be important to see how they stack up in terms of their acceptance by both the medical community and patients as a new element of standard care. If payers in the United States and other countries see that digital tools generate value, they may be more open to paying for them or be better able to articulate under what circumstances such products would be paid for.

The use of real-world data for studying digital health apps will likely present both a challenge and an opportunity. (The FDA defines real-world data as "data relating to patient health status and/or the delivery of health care routinely collected from a variety of sources" such as electronic health records, medical claims and billing data, data from product and disease registries, and patient-generated data.) Its use will be a challenge because the gold standard for regulatory decisions about new healthcare products has historically been data from randomized controlled trials. In contrast, in evaluating digital health apps, Germany's regulatory framework paves the way for the use of real-world evidence (the clinical evidence regarding the usage and potential benefits or risks of a medical product derived from analysis of real-world data). Regulators such as the FDA have acknowledged the increasingly important role that real-world data and evidence are already beginning to play in clinical studies, coverage decisions, and ongoing product monitoring, although best practices for manufacturers are only beginning to be established.

However, the opportunity to learn a great deal and to do so quickly and on an ongoing basis is an exciting feature of using real-world evidence that cannot be provided by traditional randomized controlled trials. This represents a major opportunity for all health-care decision makers—clinicians, regulators, policy makers, payers, product firms, and patients—to make more-informed and more-nimble decisions regarding which products to use and when. Moreover, the German system's performance-based reimbursement provides incentives to assess digital tools on an ongoing basis, which will generate data far beyond the one-time results derived from traditional studies.

In the longer term, digital apps' prices will be determined by their clinical performance, with real-world evidence expected to play a key role in demonstrating effectiveness.

As Germany evaluates new digital tools, it will inevitably spur the generation of a wealth of evidence that will shape the post–Covid-19 digital health ecosystem worldwide. We believe Germany's approach can be a model for other Western health-care systems that are looking to open up to digital innovation.

TAKEAWAYS

Germany's Digital Healthcare Act makes it easier to roll out new digital health tools. It includes the formalization of "prescribable applications" as well as an accelerated regulatory path for companies to take their digital health applications to market.

✓ These tools present an opportunity to assess real-world health outcomes that cannot be measured by traditional randomized controlled trials. They could help providers make better decisions regarding which products and treatments to use and when.

✓ They will produce a wealth of data on how digital tools work in practice for remote patient care, which other payers and health systems can learn from.

✓ Information gathered will be useful in convincing health-care providers of the value of digital tools, both generally and in specific use cases.

✓ Germany's approach can be a model for other health-care systems that are looking to open up to digital innovation.

Adapted from content posted on hbr.org, December 2, 2020 (product #H061RK).

BUILDING A TRANSPARENT SUPPLY CHAIN

by Vishal Gaur and Abhinav Gaiha

Blockchain, the digital record-keeping technology behind Bitcoin and other cryptocurrency networks, is a potential game changer in the financial world. But another area where it holds great promise is supply chain management. Blockchain can greatly improve supply chains by enabling faster and more cost-efficient delivery of products, enhancing products' traceability, improving coordination between partners, and aiding access to financing.

To better understand this opportunity, we studied seven major U.S. corporations that are leaders in supply chain management and are trying to figure out how blockchain can help solve the challenges they face. These companies—Corning, Emerson, Hayward, IBM, Mastercard, and two others that wish to remain anonymous—operate in varied industries: manufacturing, retailing, technology, and financial services. Some of them are just beginning to explore blockchain, a few are conducting pilots, and others have moved even further and are working with supply chain partners to develop applications. This article describes what we've learned about the state of play, the advantages that blockchain can provide, and how the use of blockchain in supply chains will differ from its use in cryptocurrencies.

A blockchain is a distributed, or decentralized, ledger—a digital system for recording transactions among multiple parties in a verifiable, tamperproof way. The ledger itself can also be programmed to trigger transactions automatically. For cryptocurrency networks that are designed to replace fiat currencies, the main function of blockchain is to enable an *unlimited* number of *anonymous* parties to transact privately and securely with one another without a central intermediary. For supply chains, it is to allow a *limited* number of *known* parties to protect their business operations against malicious actors while supporting better performance. Successful blockchain applications for supply chains will require new permissioned blockchains, new standards for representing transactions on a block, and new rules to govern the system—which are all in various stages of being developed.

The Advantages of Blockchain

Led by companies such as Walmart and Procter & Gamble, considerable advancement in supply chain information sharing has taken place since the 1990s, thanks to the use of enterprise-resource planning (ERP) systems. However, visibility remains a challenge in large supply chains involving complex transactions.

To illustrate the limitations of the current world of financial-ledger entries and ERP systems, along with the potential benefits of a world of blockchain, let us describe a hypothetical scenario: a simple transaction involving a retailer that sources a product from a supplier, and a bank that provides the working capital the supplier needs to fill the order. The transaction involves *information* flows, *inventory* flows, and *financial* flows. Note that a given flow does not result in financial-ledger entries at *all* three parties involved. And state-of-the-art ERP systems, manual audits, and inspections can't reliably connect the three flows, which makes it hard to eliminate execution errors, improve decision-making, and resolve supply chain conflicts.

Execution errors—such as mistakes in inventory data, missing shipments, and duplicate payments—are often impossible to detect in real time. Even when a problem is discovered after the fact, it is difficult and expensive to pinpoint its source or fix it by tracing the sequence of activities recorded in available ledger entries and documents. Although ERP systems capture all types of flows,

Capturing the Details of a Simple Transaction: Conventional vs. Blockchain Systems

The financial ledgers and enterprise resource planning systems now used don't reliably allow the three parties involved in a simple supply-chain transaction to see all the relevant flows of information, inventory, and money. A blockchain system eliminates the blind spots.

(Continued)

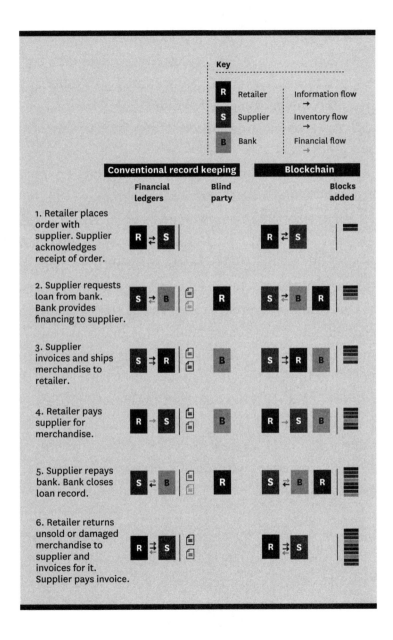

Key

R Retailer — Information flow →

S Supplier — Inventory flow →

B Bank — Financial flow →

Conventional record keeping			Blockchain
Financial ledgers	Blind party		Blocks added

1. Retailer places order with supplier. Supplier acknowledges receipt of order.

2. Supplier requests loan from bank. Bank provides financing to supplier.

3. Supplier invoices and ships merchandise to retailer.

4. Retailer pays supplier for merchandise.

5. Supplier repays bank. Bank closes loan record.

6. Retailer returns unsold or damaged merchandise to supplier and invoices for it. Supplier pays invoice.

it can be tough to assess which journal entries (accounts receivable, payments, credits for returns, and so on) correspond to which inventory transaction. This is especially true for companies engaged in thousands of transactions each day across a large network of supply chain partners and products.

Making matters worse, supply chain activities are often extremely complicated—far more so than the exhibit depicts. For example, orders, shipments, and payments may not sync up neatly, because an order may be split into several shipments and corresponding invoices, or multiple orders may be combined into a single shipment.

One common approach to improving supply chain execution is to verify transactions through audits. Auditing is necessary for ensuring compliance with contracts, but it's of limited help in improving decision-making to address operational deficiencies. Consider the problem a food company faces when its products reach the end of their shelf life in a retail store. A study that one of us (Vishal) worked on with a major manufacturer of packaged foods found that an audit or an inspection of inventory in a store can reveal the number of expired items, but it won't explain the causes. Those can include glitches in any part of the supply chain, such as inefficient inventory management upstream, suboptimal allocation of products to stores, weak or sporadic demand, and inadequate shelf rotation (failure to put older products in front of newer ones). A record of all those activities can help reduce expirations.

Another way to strengthen supply chain operations would be to mark inventory with either RFID tags or electronic product codes that adhere to GS1 standards (globally accepted rules for handling supply chain data) and to then integrate a company's ERP systems with those of its suppliers to construct a complete record of transactions. This would eliminate execution errors and improve traceability. However, the experiences of the companies we studied showed that integrating ERP systems is expensive and time-consuming. Large organizations may have more than 100 legacy ERP systems—a result of organizational changes, mergers, and acquisitions over time. Those systems often do not easily communicate with one another and may even differ in how they define data fields. One large company told us it had 17 ledgers in separate ERP systems associated with a single activity—trucking—and its suppliers and distributors had their own ledgers and ERP systems.

When blockchain record keeping is used, assets such as units of inventory, orders, loans, and bills of lading are given unique identifiers, which serve as digital tokens (similar to bitcoins). Additionally, participants in the blockchain are given unique identifiers, or digital signatures, which they use to sign the blocks they add to the blockchain. Every step of the transaction is then recorded on the blockchain as a transfer of the corresponding token from one participant to another.

Consider how the transaction in our example looks when represented on a shared blockchain (refer again to the exhibit). First, the retailer generates an order and sends it to the supplier. At this point, since no exchange of goods or services has taken place, there would be no entries in a financial ledger. However, with blockchain, the retailer records the digital token for the order. The supplier then logs in the order and confirms to the retailer that the order has been received—an action that again gets recorded on the blockchain but would not generate an entry in a financial ledger. Next the supplier requests a working-capital loan from the bank to finance the production of the goods. The bank verifies the order on the shared blockchain, approves the loan, and records the loan's digital token on the same blockchain. And so on.

A blockchain is valuable partly because it comprises a chronological string of blocks integrating all three types of flows in the transaction and captures details that aren't recorded in a financial-ledger system. Moreover, each block is encrypted and distributed to all participants, who maintain their own copies of the blockchain. Thanks to these features, the blockchain provides a complete, trustworthy, and tamperproof audit trail of the three categories of activities in the supply chain.

Blockchain thus greatly reduces, if not eliminates, the kind of execution, traceability, and coordination problems that we've discussed. Since participants have their own individual copies of the blockchain, each party can review the status of a transaction, identify errors, and hold counterparties responsible for their actions. No participant can overwrite past data because doing so would entail having to rewrite all subsequent blocks on all shared copies of the blockchain.

The bank in our example can also use the blockchain to improve supply chain financing. It can make better lending decisions because by viewing the blockchain, it can verify the transactions between the supplier and the retailer without having to conduct physical audits and financial reviews, which are tedious and error-prone processes. And including lending records in the blockchain, along with data about invoicing, payments, and the physical movement of goods, can make transactions more cost-effective, easier to audit, and less risky for all participants.

Furthermore, many of these functions can be automated through *smart contracts*, in which lines of computer code use data from the blockchain to verify when contractual obligations have been met and payments can be issued. Smart contracts can be programmed to assess the status of a transaction and automatically take actions such as releasing a payment, recording ledger entries, and flagging exceptions in need of manual intervention.

It's important to note that a blockchain would not replace the broad range of transaction-processing, accounting, and management-control functions performed by ERP systems, such as invoicing, payment, and reporting. Indeed, the encrypted linked list or chainlike data structure of a blockchain is not suited for fast storage and retrieval—or even efficient storage. Instead, the blockchain would interface with legacy systems across participating firms. Each firm would generate blocks of transactions from its internal ERP system and add them to the blockchain. This would make it easy to integrate various flows of transactions across firms.

The Applications

Let's now take an in-depth look at how the companies we studied are applying blockchain to tackle needs that current technologies and methods can't address.

Enhancing traceability

The U.S. Drug Supply Chain Security Act of 2013 requires pharmaceutical companies to identify and trace prescription drugs to protect consumers from counterfeit, stolen, or harmful products. Driven by that mandate, a large pharmaceutical company in our study is collaborating with its supply chain partners to use blockchain for this purpose. Drug inventory is tagged with electronic product codes that adhere to GS1 standards. As each unit of inventory flows from one firm to another, its tag is scanned and recorded on the blockchain, creating a history of each item all the way through the supply chain—from its source to the end consumer. Some early success in piloting this approach in the United States has led the company to conduct more pilots in other locations and to move toward broad implementation in Europe. Meanwhile, IBM is working on a similar effort to create a safer food supply chain. It has founded the IBM Food Trust and entered into a partnership with Walmart to use blockchain for tracing fresh produce and other food products.

These kinds of applications require minimal sharing of information: Purchase orders, invoices, and payments do not need to be included on the same blockchain. As a result, companies that are wary of sharing competitive data are more willing to participate on the platform.

The benefits are clear. If a company discovers a faulty product, the blockchain enables the firm and its supply chain partners to trace the product, identify all suppliers involved with it, identify production and shipment batches associated with it, and efficiently recall it. If a product is perishable (as fresh produce and certain drugs are), the blockchain lets participating companies monitor quality automatically: A refrigerated container equipped with an Internet of Things (IoT) device to monitor the temperature can record any unsafe fluctuations on the blockchain. And if there are concerns about the authenticity of a product that a retailer returns, the blockchain can allay them, because counterfeit goods would lack a verification history on the blockchain. (We'll talk later about how companies are trying to prevent corrupt actors from introducing counterfeit goods into both supply chains and their blockchains.) Companies across industries are therefore exploring this application of blockchain—motivated either by regulations requiring them to demonstrate the provenance of their products or by downstream customers seeking the capability to trace component inventory.

Increasing efficiency and speed and reducing disruptions

Emerson, a multinational manufacturing and engineering company, has a complex supply chain. It involves thousands of components across many suppliers, customers, and locations. Michael Train, the president of Emerson, told us that such supply chains often have to contend with long, unpredictable lead times and lack of visibility. As a result, a small delay or disruption in any part of the supply chain can lead to excess inventory and stock-outs in other parts. He believes that blockchain could help overcome these challenges.

Here's a simple illustration of the problem and how blockchain could address it. Consider product A, which uses components C1 and C2, and product B, which uses components C1 and C3. If the manufacture of product B is held up because of a disruption in the production of component C3, the optimal move is to temporarily allocate inventory of C1 to product A until the disruption is resolved. However, if all products and components are manufactured by different companies with limited visibility into one another's inventory, what could easily happen is that excess inventory of C1 piles up at the company making product B even if the maker of product A has a stock-out of C1.

One solution is for the companies in question to agree to centralize their data on production and inventory-allocation decisions in a common repository. But imagine the level of integration that would entail: All involved companies would have to trust the others with their data and accept centralized decisions, regardless of whether they are partners or competitors. That's not realistic.

A more practical solution is for participating companies to share their inventory flows on a blockchain and allow each company to make its own decisions, using common, complete information. Companies would utilize a kanban system to place orders with one another and manage production. Kanban cards would be assigned to the produced items, and the blockchain would record digital tokens representing the kanban cards. This would enhance the visibility of inventory flows across companies and make lead times more predictable.

Emerson is not the only company that thinks blockchain could increase the efficiency and speed of its supply chain. So does Hayward, a multinational manufacturer of swimming pool equipment. (Disclosure: Vishal has done a small amount of consulting for Hayward. He has also been hired to advise a startup that's developing blockchain applications for the palm oil industry.) According to Don Smith, Hayward's senior vice president of operations, it is possible to treat finished goods, process capacity, work-in-process inventory, and raw materials like digital currency. If you do, he says, machine time and inventory at various stages can be reliably assigned to customer orders. Blockchain makes this possible by solving the double-spend problem—the erroneous allocation of the same unit of capacity or inventory to two different orders.

Walmart Canada has already begun using blockchain with the trucking companies that transport its inventory. A shared blockchain makes it possible to synchronize logistics data, track shipments, and automate payments without requiring significant changes to the trucking firms' internal processes or information technology systems.

Part of the appeal of using blockchain to enhance supply chain efficiency and speed is that these applications, much like those for improving traceability, require participating companies to share only limited data—in this case, just inventory or shipment data. Moreover, these applications are useful even within large organizations with multiple ERP systems.

Improving financing, contracting, and international transactions

When inventory, information, and financial flows are shared among firms through a blockchain, significant gains in supply chain financing, contracting, and doing business internationally are possible.

Consider the matter of financing. Banks that provide working capital and trade credit to firms face a well-known problem of information asymmetry regarding a borrower firm's business, the quality of its assets, and its liabilities. For example, a company might borrow money from several banks against the same asset, or request a loan for one purpose and then use it for another. Banks design their processes to control such risks, which increases transaction costs, slows down access to capital, and reduces the capital available to small firms. Such frictions are detrimental not only to banks but also to firms that need cheap working capital.

Another activity ripe for improvement is accounts payable management, an elaborate process that involves invoicing, reconciling invoices against purchase orders, keeping track of terms and payments, and conducting reviews and approvals at each step. Even though ERP systems have automated many of these steps, considerable manual intervention is still needed. And since neither of the transacting firms has complete information, conflicts often arise.

A third area of opportunity is cross-border trade, which involves manual processes, physical documents, many intermediaries, and multiple checks and verifications at ports of entry and exit. Transactions are slow, costly, and plagued by low visibility into the status of shipments.

The retailing and financial services companies we studied are conducting pilot blockchain projects or developing platforms in all three areas. By connecting inventory, information, and financial flows and sharing them with all transacting parties, a blockchain enables companies to reconcile purchase orders, invoices, and payments much more easily and to track the progress of a transaction with counterparties. When the supplier receives an order, a bank with access to the blockchain can immediately provide the supplier with working capital, and when merchandise is delivered to the buyer, the bank can promptly obtain payments. Since there is a readily available audit trail and reconciliations can be automated, using smart applications that rely on the blockchain data, conflicts between the bank and the borrowing firm are eliminated.

Creating a Workable Technology

The companies we studied have found that using blockchain in supply chain management will require the creation of new rules, because the needs of supply chains differ from those of cryptocurrency networks in important ways. The blockchain protocol for the Bitcoin network is a marvelous system that simultaneously achieves several goals. It provides a remarkably secure, irrevocable record of financial transactions, minimizes the double-spend problem, and provides proof of ownership of a digital coin. And it does so without relying on a centralized authority and while allowing participants to remain anonymous and enter and exit the network freely. To achieve all this, however, the Bitcoin network sacrifices speed, consumes a large amount of energy to mine bitcoins, and has some vulnerability to hacking.

Supply chains do not need to make the same trade-offs because they operate in a different way and have different characteristics. Let's examine those in depth.

Known participants

Supply chains require private blockchains among known parties, not open blockchains among anonymous users. So that members of a supply chain can ascertain the source and quality of their inventory, each unit of it must be firmly coupled with the identity of its particular owner at every step along the way. Consequently, only known parties can be allowed to participate in such a blockchain, which means that companies must receive permission to join the system.

Moreover, permission must be granted selectively. That's because the open and decentralized structure of block-chain poses a risk to data privacy. When companies post transactions on a blockchain, that data can be accessed by any participant. As the volume of data swells, it could potentially be misused to gather competitive intelligence, trade stocks, or predict market movements. For security reasons, therefore, the blockchain participants need to be vetted and approved.

Building a trusted group of partners with which to share data on a blockchain will entail overcoming several challenges. One is the need for a governance mechanism to determine the rules of the system, such as who can be invited to join the network, what data is shared, how it is encrypted, who has access, how disputes will be resolved, and what the scope is for the use of IoT and smart contracts. Another challenge is figuring out how to address the impact that blockchain could have on pricing and inventory-allocation decisions by making information about the quantity or age of products in the supply chain more transparent. It's hard to predict where in the supply chain the costs and benefits of this transparency will fall.

For these reasons, the companies that we studied were focusing on narrow applications such as the traceability of drugs and food products and the management of accounts payable—applications that are supported by well-defined use cases or regulatory requirements. Firms limit the types of information recorded on the blockchain to reduce the risk to data privacy and make the system more readily acceptable to supply chain partners.

Simpler consensus protocols

Blockchain requires a consensus protocol—some mechanism for maintaining a single version of the history of transactions that is agreed to by everyone. Since cryptocurrency networks are peer-to-peer without a central authority, they use a complex method called *proof of work*. It ensures that all transactions on the network are accepted by the majority of participants, but unfortunately, it also limits the speed at which new blocks can be added. Consequently, it is too slow to handle the speed and volume of transactions in supply chains.

Consider the pharmaceutical industry, where 4 billion salable units enter the drug supply chain every year in the United States. Each unit is handled three to five times, on average. That translates to roughly 33 million to 55 million transactions a day, on average. The Bitcoin network, in contrast, allows only about 360,000 transactions a day.

Fortunately, if a blockchain is permissioned and private, the proof-of-work method is not necessary to establish consensus. Simpler methods can be used to determine who has the right to add the next block to the blockchain. One such method is a *round-robin protocol*, where the right to add a block rotates among the participants in a fixed order. Since all participants are known, a malicious actor would be discovered if it used its turn to modify the chain in a harmful or illegitimate way. And disputes can be resolved easily by participants' validating previous blocks.

Security of physical assets

Even when a blockchain record is secure, there is still the danger that a contaminated or counterfeit product might be tagged and introduced into the supply chain, either in error or by a corrupt actor. Another danger is inaccurate inventory data resulting from mistakes in scanning, tagging, and data entry.

Companies are addressing these risks in three ways. First, they are stringently conducting physical audits when products first enter the supply chain to ensure that shipments match blockchain records. Second, they are building distributed applications, called dApps, that track products throughout the supply chain, check data integrity, and communicate with the blockchain to prevent errors and deception. If a counterfeit or an error is detected, it can be traced to its source using the blockchain trail of the transactions for that asset. Third, companies are making the blockchain more robust by using IoT devices and sensors to automatically scan products and add records to the blockchain without human intervention.

One area where tokenization is sufficient to provide trust and security is the trading of assets like digital books and music. If the ownership of these assets is tied to a blockchain platform, counterfeits can be completely eliminated. For instance, universities commonly use digital reading packets for many courses, working in partnership with publishers and copyright owners. Significant efficiency gains could be generated by knitting this digital supply chain into a blockchain platform with smart contracts that can help participants access products, verify ownership, and handle payment.

. . .

There is considerable room to improve supply chains in terms of end-to-end traceability, speed of product delivery, coordination, and financing. Blockchain can be a powerful tool for addressing the deficiencies, as the companies we studied have proved. It is now time for supply chain managers who are standing on the sidelines to assess the potential of blockchain for their businesses. They need to join the efforts to develop new rules, experiment with different technologies, conduct pilots with various blockchain platforms, and build an ecosystem with other firms. Yes, this will require a commitment of resources, but the investment promises to generate a handsome return.

TAKEAWAYS

Supply chain management is one of the most promising applications of blockchain technology. Blockchain can help partners create a complete, transparent, tamperproof history of information flows, inventory flows, and financial flows in transactions.

✓ Blockchain can enable faster and more cost-efficient product delivery, make products more traceable, streamline the financing process, and enhance coordination.

✓ Using blockchain in supply chain management requires: restricting participation to known, trusted partners; adopting a new consensus protocol; and taking steps to keep errors and counterfeits out of the supply chain.

✓ If implemented thoughtfully, blockchain could pay big dividends for companies in a host of industries.

Adapted from Harvard Business Review, *May–June 2020 (product #R2003F).*

Section 2

LOOKING AHEAD TO FUTURE TECH

5

WHAT BRAIN-COMPUTER INTERFACES COULD MEAN FOR THE FUTURE OF WORK

by Alexandre Gonfalonieri

I magine if your manager could know whether you actually paid attention in your last Zoom meeting. Or, imagine if you could prepare your next presentation using only your thoughts. These scenarios might soon become a reality thanks to the development of brain-computer interfaces (BCIs).

In the simplest terms, think of a BCI as a bridge between your brain and an external device. As of today, we mostly rely on electroencephalography (EEG)—a collection of methods for monitoring the electrical activity of the brain—to create that bridge. But that's changing. By leveraging multiple sensors and complex algorithms, it's becoming possible to analyze brain signals and extract relevant brain patterns. Brain activity can then be recorded by a noninvasive device—no surgical intervention needed. In fact, the majority of existing and mainstream BCIs are noninvasive, such as wearable headbands and earbuds.

The development of BCI technology was initially focused on helping paralyzed people control assistive devices using their thoughts. But new use cases are being identified all the time. For example, BCIs can now be used as a neurofeedback training tool to improve cognitive performance. I expect to see a growing number of professionals leveraging BCI tools to improve their performance at work. Your BCI could detect that your attention level is too low compared with the importance of a given meeting or task and trigger an alert. It could also adapt the lighting of your office based on how stressed you are, or it could prevent you from using your company car if it detects drowsiness.

Muse, a Toronto-based startup, has developed a sensing headband that gives real-time information about what's going on in your brain. It even has a corporate wellness program that promises to "help your employees lower stress, increase resilience, and improve their engagement." Other headbands on the market also use proprietary sensors to detect brain signals and leverage machine-learning algorithms to provide insights into the engagement levels of users/workers. The headbands can track whether someone is focused or distracted. Theoretically, this could help individuals with day-to-day tasks by evaluating which ones should be tackled first based on the user's attention level. But there's also huge potential for abuse, which I'll further explore below.

This ability to monitor (and potentially control) attention levels creates new possibilities for managers. For example, companies could have access to a specific BCI HR dashboard, in which all employees' brain data would be displayed, in real time. Are we going to see supervisors monitoring the attention levels of their colleagues? At the end of each annual performance review, are we going to also analyze and compare attention levels thanks to our BCIs? Your brain information may be of interest to your employer, allowing them to keep an eye on how focused you are, and allowing them to adapt your workload accordingly—again, creating the possibility for misuse.

I also expect more professional events to leverage BCIs in the near future. Indeed, research has shown that brain data can help predict which booths and activities people would visit.[1] In the future, are we going to need BCIs to participate in business events?

Beyond the analysis of brain signals, some companies are already working on solutions that can actually modulate your brain activity. Researchers at Columbia University have shown how neurofeedback using an EEG-based BCI could be used to affect alertness and to improve subjects' performance in a cognitively demanding task.[2] Despite these promising results, some experts, such as Theodore Zanto, a director of the University of California, San Francisco neuroscience program, say that while BCIs based on EEG scans can determine a user's attention levels, they are not yet capable of differentiating what the user is actually focused on. In a January 2019 *Medium* article, Zanto says, "I haven't seen any data indicating you can dissociate if someone is paying attention to the teacher or their phone or just their own internal thoughts and daydreaming."[3] Moreover, I realized through my own work that BCIs are also affected by a user's specific characteristics, such as gender, age, and lifestyle. Indeed, my team and I are trying to determine how brain activity can affect an athlete's performance. According to some research, "psychological factors including attention, memory load, fatigue, and competing cognitive processes, as well as users' basic characteristics such as lifestyle, gender, and age, influence instantaneous brain dynamics."[4]

Experts believe that around "15% to 30% of individuals are inherently not able to produce brain signals robust enough to operate a BCI."[5] Obviously, this situation can lead to wrong results and ultimately bad decisions from companies. BCIs still have a long way to go, and much improvement is needed.

Another use case for BCIs at work is related to the ways we interact with machines and devices. In fact, I predict that in the future, the most "dangerous" jobs will *require* the use of BCIs. For example, some BCI companies have already used EEG to analyze signals of drowsy driving. Companies with workers who operate dangerous machinery may require their workers to be monitored in the same way. I believe that eventually it will be mandatory for pilots and surgeons to wear a BCI while working.

The idea of humans interacting with devices is a pillar of BCIs, as BCI technology provides direct communication between the brain and external devices. In the next few years, we might be able to control a PowerPoint presentation or Excel file using only our brains. Some prototypes can translate brain activity into text or instructions for a computer, and in theory, as the technology improves, we'll see people using BCIs to write memos or reports at work.

We could also imagine a work environment that adapts automatically to an employee's stress level or thoughts.

BCIs can detect the mental state of a worker and adjust nearby devices accordingly (smart home utilization). For example, when stressed, your headband could send information (using Bluetooth) to your computer so that it starts playing your "calm" playlist, or it could trigger Slack to turn to "do not disturb" mode while automatically canceling your next appointment. Obviously, this scenario raises questions about privacy. Would you feel comfortable knowing that others can know precisely how you feel mentally? What if this information could be used against you? What if this data could be modified by someone else without your approval?

Researchers are also experimenting with "pass-thoughts" as alternatives to passwords. Soon we might log into our various devices and platforms using our thoughts. As described in this *IEEE Spectrum* article, "When we perform mental tasks like picturing a shape or singing a song in our heads, our brains generate unique neuronal electrical signals. A billion people could mentally hum the same song and no two brain-wave patterns generated by that task would be alike. An electroencephalograph (EEG) would read those brain waves using noninvasive electrodes that record the signals. The unique patterns can be used like a password or biometric identification."[6]

As you can imagine, there are myriad ethical questions and concerns surrounding the use of BCI technology in the workplace. Companies who opt to use BCI technology can face massive backlash from employees, not to mention from the public. When it comes to collecting brain data, the potential for abuse is frightening: Even when used with the best of intentions, companies could risk becoming overly dependent on using brain data to evaluate, monitor, and train employees, and there are risks associated with that.

BCIs aren't a perfect technology—there's no telling what sort of mistakes or mishaps we'll encounter as companies and individuals begin to use these devices in the real world. What's more, BCIs—like any technology—can be hacked. Hackers can access a BCI headband and create or send manipulated EEG data. A hacker could also intercept and alter all data transmitted by your BCI. It's possible that a hacker could steal your passthought user credentials and interact with your devices (laptop, car, etc.). These risks can directly impact your physical integrity. Brain data could also be stolen and used against you for extortion purposes. The potential for serious abuse is significant. When companies begin to use and analyze brain data, how will they prioritize privacy and data security and meet the industry's top standards for protecting employee data? Who will ultimately own the data that's collected? And what are employees' rights when their companies begin to roll out these technologies?

Obviously, the technology is well ahead of the policies and regulations that need to be put in place.

Still, the technology is slowly moving into the mass market. A growing number of startups and large tech firms are working on safer, more accurate, and cheaper BCIs. I expect to see business leaders embracing this technology and trying to leverage brain data to achieve better work efficiency and greater safety. I recommend that business leaders start building a BCI strategy as soon as possible to address the potential risks and benefits.

Brain-computer interfaces are slowly moving into the mass market, and a growing number of startups and large tech firms are working on safer, more accurate, and cheaper BCIs. To ensure your company is keeping up with the benefits and potential risks, start building a BCI strategy as soon as possible.

✓ Companies may one day use BCI technology to monitor the attention levels and mental states of their employees.

✓ BCIs could also be used for safety or mental health, such as preventing you from using your company car if you are too drowsy or automatically adjusting nearby devices according to your stress level or thoughts.

✓ BCIs might soon allow us to control computer functions by merely thinking.

✓ Questions surrounding data privacy and ethics abound in the discussion of BCIs, and the technology is well ahead of policies and regulations that need to be put in place.

NOTES

1. Michele W. Berger, "A Wearable New Technology Moves Brain Monitoring from the Lab to the Real Word," *Penn Today*, August 13, 2019, https://penntoday.upenn.edu/news/innovative -technology-wearable-portable-EEG-moves-brain-monitoring -from-lab-to-real-world.

2. Josef Faller, Jennifer Cummings, Sameer Saproo, and Paul Sajda, "Regulation of Arousal via Online Neurofeedback Improves Human Performance in a Demanding Sensory-Motor Task," *Proceedings of the National Academy of Sciences of the United States of America*, March 12, 2019, https://www.pnas.org/content/116/13 /6482.

3. Daniel Sun, "The New Focus 1 Headband," Neurotech@Berkeley, January 15, 2019, https://medium.com/neurotech-berkeley/the -new-focus-1-headband-c441123af668.

4. Simanto Saha, Khondaker A. Mamun, Khawza Ahmed, Raq-ibul Mostafa, Ganesh R. Naik, Ahsan Khandoker, Sam Darvishi, and Mathias Baumert, "Progress in Brain Computer Interfaces: Challenges and Trends," *Frontiers in Systems Neuroscience*, February 25, 2021, https://www.frontiersin.org/articles/10.3389/fnsys.2021.578875/full.

5. Carmen Vidaurre and Benjamin Blankertz, "Towards a Cure for BCI Illiteracy," *Brain Topography* 23, no. 2 (2010), 194–198, https://www.ncbi.nlm.nih.gov/pmc/articles/PMC2874052/.

6. Emily Waltz, "From Passwords to Passthoughts: Logging In to Your Devices with Your Mind," *IEEE Spectrum*, August 31, 2016, https://spectrum.ieee.org/the-human-os/biomedical/devices/logging-into-your-devices-with-your-mind.

Adapted from content posted on hbr.org, October 6, 2020 (product #H05WH0).

GET READY FOR THE QUANTUM COMPUTING REVOLUTION

by Shohini Ghose

Quantum physics has already changed our lives. Thanks to the invention of the laser and the transistor—both products of quantum theory—almost every electronic device we use today is an example of quantum physics in action. We may now be on the brink of a second quantum revolution as we attempt to harness even more of the power of the quantum world. Quantum computing and quantum communication could impact many sectors, including health care, energy, finance, security, and entertainment. Recent studies predict a multibillion-dollar quantum industry by 2030.[1] However, significant practical challenges need to be overcome before this level of large-scale impact is achievable.

Quantum Versus Classical

Although quantum theory is over a century old, the current quantum revolution is based on the more recent realization that uncertainty—a fundamental property of quantum particles—can be a powerful resource. At the level of individual quantum particles, such as electrons or photons (particles of light), it's impossible to precisely know every property of the particle at any given moment in time. For example, the GPS in your car can tell you your location and your speed and direction all at once, and precisely enough to get you to your destination. But a quantum GPS could not simultaneously and precisely display all those properties of an electron—not because of faulty design but because the laws of quantum physics forbid it. In the quantum world, we must use the language of probability, rather than certainty. And in the context of computing based on binary digits (bits) of 0s and 1s, this means that quantum bits (qubits) have some likelihood of being 1 and some likelihood of being 0 at the same time.

Such imprecision is at first disconcerting. In our everyday classical computers, 0s and 1s are associated with switches and electronic circuits turning on and off. Not knowing exactly if they are on or off wouldn't make much sense from a computing point of view. In fact, that would lead to errors in calculations. But the revolutionary idea behind quantum information processing is that quantum uncertainty—a fuzzy, in-between "superposition" of 0 and 1—is actually not a bug but a feature. It provides new levers for more-powerful ways to communicate and process data.

Quantum Communication and Quantum Computing in Action

One outcome of the probabilistic nature of quantum theory is that quantum information cannot be precisely copied. From a security lens, this is game-changing. Hackers trying to copy quantum keys used for encrypting and transmitting messages would be foiled, even if they had access to a quantum computer or other powerful resources. This fundamentally unhackable encryption is based on the laws of physics, not on the complex mathematical algorithms used today. While mathematical encryption techniques are vulnerable to being cracked by powerful enough computers, cracking quantum encryption would require violating the laws of physics.

Just as quantum encryption is fundamentally different from current encryption methods based on mathematical complexity, quantum computers are fundamentally different from current classical computers. The two are as different as a car and a horse and cart. A car is based on harnessing different laws of physics compared to a horse and cart. It gets you to your destination faster and to new destinations previously out of reach. The same can be said for a quantum computer compared to a classical computer. A quantum computer harnesses the probabilistic laws of quantum physics to process data and perform computations in a novel way. It can complete certain computing tasks faster, and it can perform new, previously impossible tasks, such as, for example, quantum teleportation, where information encoded in quantum particles disappears in one location and is exactly (but not instantaneously) re-created in another location far away. While that sounds like sci-fi, this new form of data transmission could be a vital component of a future quantum internet.

A particularly important application of quantum computers might be to simulate and analyze molecules for drug development and materials design. A quantum computer is uniquely suited for such tasks because it would operate on the same laws of quantum physics as the molecules it is simulating. Using a quantum device to simulate quantum chemistry could be far more efficient than using the fastest classical supercomputers today.

Quantum computers are also ideally suited for solving complex optimization tasks and performing fast searches of unsorted data. This could be relevant for many applications, from sorting climate data or health or financial data, to optimizing supply chain logistics, workforce management, or traffic flow.

Preparing for the Quantum Future

The quantum race is already underway. Governments and private investors all around the world are pouring billions of dollars into quantum research and development. Satellite-based quantum key distribution for encryption has been demonstrated, laying the groundwork for a potential quantum-security-based global communication network. IBM, Google, Microsoft, Amazon, and other companies are investing heavily in developing large-scale quantum-computing hardware and software. Nobody is quite there yet. While small-scale quantum computers are operational today, a major hurdle to scaling up the technology is the issue of dealing with errors. Compared to bits, qubits are incredibly fragile. Even the slightest disturbance from the outside world is enough to destroy quantum information. That's why most current machines need to be carefully shielded in isolated environments operating at temperatures far colder than outer space. While a theoretical framework for quantum error correction has been developed, implementing it in an energy- and resource-efficient manner poses significant engineering challenges.

Given the current state of the field, it's not clear when or if the full power of quantum computing will be accessible. Even so, business leaders should consider developing strategies to address three main areas:

1. **Planning for quantum security:** Current data-encryption protocols are vulnerable not only to future quantum computers but also to ever-more-powerful classical computers. New standards for encryption (whether classical or quantum) are inevitable. Changing over to a quantum-secure architecture and supporting infrastructure for data security will require planning, resources, and quantum expertise. Even if quantum computers may be a decade away, waiting until then to adapt would be too late. The time to start the process is now.

2. **Identifying use cases:** Nobody could have predicted the myriad ways that classical computers impact every aspect of our lives. Predicting quantum

applications is equally challenging. That's why, in order to fully tap into the potential of quantum computing, business leaders and experts in different sectors such as health, finance, or energy must connect with quantum researchers and hardware and software engineers. This will facilitate the development of industry-specific quantum solutions tailored for currently available quantum technologies or for future scalable quantum computing. Interdisciplinary expertise and training will be critical to building and growing the quantum app store.

3. **Thinking through responsible design:** Who will develop and have access to quantum technology, and how will users engage with it? The impact of AI and blockchain has demonstrated the need to consider the social, ethical, and environmental implications of new technologies. It's early days for the quantum industry. That provides a rare opportunity to embed inclusive practices from the start and build a responsible and sustainable road map for quantum computing.

The rapid growth in the quantum tech sector over the past five years has been exciting. But the future remains unpredictable. Luckily, quantum theory tells us that unpredictability is not necessarily a bad thing. In fact, two qubits can be locked together in such a way that individually they remain undetermined, but jointly they are perfectly in sync—either both qubits are 0 or both are 1. This combination of joint certainty and individual unpredictability—a phenomenon called entanglement—is a powerful fuel that drives many quantum computing algorithms. Perhaps it also holds a lesson for how to build a quantum industry. By planning responsibly while also embracing future uncertainty, businesses can improve their odds of being ready for the quantum future.

R&D for quantum computing and communication is accelerating. Although the technology is years away from practical applications, consider developing strategies to address three main areas of the quantum future:

✓ **Planning for quantum security.** Current data-encryption protocols will be vulnerable not only to future quantum computers but also to ever-more-powerful classical computers. New standards for encryption are inevitable.

✓ **Identifying use cases for quantum computing.** Promising applications include simulating and analyzing molecules for drug development and materials design; solving complex optimization tasks; and performing fast searches of unsorted data.

✓ **Thinking through responsible design.** It's early days for the quantum industry, providing a rare opportunity to embed inclusive practices from the start and build a responsible and sustainable road map.

NOTE

1. Quantum Analyst, "Quantum Computing Market Size: Superpositioned for Growth?" *The Quantum Daily*, February 18, 2020, https://thequantumdaily.com/2020/02/18/the-quantum -computing-market-size-superpositioned-for-growth/.

Adapted from "Are You Ready for the Quantum Computing Revolution?" on hbr .org, September 17, 2020 (product #H05VI7).

THE COMMERCIAL SPACE AGE IS HERE

by Matt Weinzierl and Mehak Sarang

T here's no shortage of hype surrounding the commercial space industry. But while tech leaders promise us moon bases and settlements on Mars, the space economy has thus far remained distinctly local—at least in a cosmic sense. In 2020, however, we crossed an important threshold: For the first time in human history, humans accessed space via a vehicle built and owned not by any government but by a private corporation with its sights set on affordable space settlement. It was the first significant step toward building an economy both *in* space and *for* space. The implications—for business, policy, and society at large—are hard to overstate.

In 2019, 95% of the estimated $366 billion in revenue earned in the space sector was from the *space-for-earth* economy: that is, goods or services produced in space for use on earth. The space-for-earth economy includes telecommunications and internet infrastructure, earth observation capabilities, national security satellites, and more. This economy is booming, and though research shows that it faces the challenges of overcrowding and monopolization that tend to arise whenever companies compete for a scarce natural resource, projections for its future are optimistic.[1] Decreasing costs for launch and space hardware in general have enticed new entrants into this market, and companies in a variety of industries have already begun leveraging satellite technology and access to space to drive innovation and efficiency in their bound-for-earth products and services.

In contrast, the *space-for-space* economy—that is, goods and services produced in space for use in space, such as mining the moon or asteroids for material with which to construct in-space habitats or supply refueling depots—has struggled to get off the ground. As far back as the 1970s, research commissioned by NASA predicted the rise of a space-based economy that would supply the demands of hundreds, thousands, even millions of humans living in space, dwarfing the space-for-earth economy (and eventually the entire terrestrial economy as well).[2] The realization of such a vision would change how all of us do business, live our lives, and govern our societies—but to date, we've never even had more than 13 people in space at one time, leaving that dream as little more than science fiction.

Today, however, there is reason to think that we may finally be reaching the first stages of a true space-for-space economy. SpaceX's recent achievements (in cooperation with NASA), as well as upcoming efforts by Boeing, Blue Origin, and Virgin Galactic to put people in space sustainably and at scale, mark the opening of a new chapter of spaceflight led by private firms. These firms have both the intention and capability to bring private citizens to space as passengers, tourists, and—eventually—settlers, opening the door for businesses to start meeting the demand those people create over the next several decades with an array of space-for-space goods and services.

Welcome to the (Commercial) Space Age

In our research, we examined how the model of centralized, government-directed human space activity born in the 1960s has, over the last two decades, made way for a new model, in which public initiatives in space increasingly share the stage with private priorities.[3] Centralized, government-led space programs will inevitably focus on space-for-earth activities that are in the public interest, such as national security, basic science, and national pride. This is only natural, as expenditures for these programs must be justified by demonstrating benefits for citizens—and the citizens these governments represent are (nearly) all on Earth.

In contrast to governments, the private sector is eager to put people in space to pursue their own personal interests, not the state's—and then supply the demand they create. This is the vision driving SpaceX, which in its first 20 years has entirely upended the rocket launch industry, securing 60% of the global commercial launch market and building ever-larger spacecraft designed to ferry passengers not just to the International Space Station (ISS) but also to its own promised settlement on Mars.

Today, the space-for-space market is limited to supplying the people who are already in space: that is, the handful of astronauts employed by NASA and other government programs. While SpaceX has grand visions of supporting large numbers of private space travelers, their current space-for-space activities have all been in response to demand from government customers (i.e., NASA). But as decreasing launch costs enable companies like SpaceX to leverage economies of scale and put more people into space, growing private-sector demand (that is, tourists and settlers, rather than government employees) could turn these proof-of-concept initiatives into a sustainable, large-scale industry.

This model—of selling to NASA with the hopes of eventually creating and expanding into a larger private market—is exemplified by SpaceX, but the company is by no means the only player taking this approach. For instance, while SpaceX is focused on space-for-space transportation, another key component of this burgeoning industry will be manufacturing.

Made In Space, Inc. has been at the forefront of manufacturing "in space, for space" since 2014, when it 3D-printed a wrench on board the ISS. Today, the company is exploring other products, such as high-quality fiber-optic cable, that terrestrial customers may be willing to pay to have manufactured in zero gravity. But the company also recently received a $74 million contract to 3D-print large metal beams in space for use on NASA spacecraft, and future private-sector spacecraft will certainly have similar manufacturing needs, which Made In Space hopes to be well positioned to fulfill. Just as SpaceX has begun by supplying NASA but hopes to eventually serve a much larger, private-sector market, Made In Space's current work with NASA could be the first step along a path toward supporting a variety of private-sector manufacturing applications for which the costs of manufacturing on Earth and transporting into space would be prohibitive.

Another major area of space-for-space investment is in building and operating space infrastructure such as habitats, laboratories, and factories. Axiom Space, a current leader in this field, recently announced that it would be flying the "first fully private commercial mission to space" in 2022 on board SpaceX's Crew Dragon capsule. Axiom was also awarded a contract for exclusive access to a module of the ISS, facilitating its plans to develop modules for commercial activity on the station (and eventually, beyond it).

This infrastructure is likely to spur investment in a wide array of complementary services to supply the demand of the people living and working within it. For example, in February 2020, Maxar Technologies was awarded a $142 million contract from NASA to develop a robotic construction tool that would be assembled in space for use on low-Earth-orbit spacecraft. Private-sector spacecraft or settlements will no doubt have need for a variety of similar construction and repair tools.

And of course, the private sector isn't just about industrial products. Creature comforts also promise to be an area of rapid growth, as companies endeavor to support the human side of life in the harsh environment of space. In 2015, for example, Argotec and Lavazza collaborated to build an espresso machine that could function in the zero-gravity environment of the ISS, delivering a bit of everyday luxury to the crew.

To be sure, for half a century people have dreamt of using the vacuum and weightlessness of space to source or make things that cannot be made on Earth, and time and again the business case has failed to pan out. Skepticism is natural. Those failures, however, have been in space-for-earth applications. For example, two startups of the 2010s, Planetary Resources and Deep Space Industries, recognized the potential of space mining early on. But for both companies, the lack of a space-for-space economy meant that their near-term survival depended on selling mined material—precious metals or rare elements—to earthbound customers. When it became clear that demand was insufficient to justify the high costs, funding dried up, and both companies pivoted to other ventures.

These were failures of space-for-earth business models—but the demand for in-space mining of raw building material, metals, and water will be enormous once humans are living in space (and therefore far cheaper to supply). In other words, when people are living and working in space, we are likely to look back on these early asteroid-mining companies less as failures and more as simply ahead of their time.

Seizing the Space-for-Space Opportunity

The opportunity presented by the space-for-space economy is huge—but it could easily be missed. To seize this moment, policy makers must provide regulatory and institutional frameworks that will enable the risk-taking and innovation necessary for a decentralized, private-sector-driven space economy. We believe three specific policy areas will be especially important:

1. Enabling private individuals to take on greater risk than would be tolerable for government-employed astronauts. First, as part of a general shift to that more decentralized, market-oriented space sector, policy makers should consider allowing private space tourists and settlers to voluntarily take on more risk than states would tolerate for government-employed astronauts. In the long run, ensuring high safety levels will be essential to convince larger numbers of people to travel or live in space, but in the early years of exploration, too great an aversion to risk will stop progress before it starts.

An instructive analogy can be found in how NASA works with its contractors: In the mid-2000s, NASA shifted from using cost-plus contracts (in which NASA shouldered all the economic risk of investing in space) to fixed-price contracts (in which risk was distributed between NASA and their contractors). Because of private companies' greater tolerance for risk, this shift catalyzed a burst of activity in the sector—sometimes referred to as "New Space." A similar shift in how we approach voluntary risk-taking by private-sector astronauts may be necessary in order to launch the space-for-space economy.

2. Judiciously implementing government regulation and support.

Second, as with most markets, developing a stable space economy will depend on judicious government regulation and support. NASA and the U.S. Commerce and State Departments' recommitment to "create a regulatory environment in [low-Earth orbit] that enables American commercial activities to thrive" is a good sign that the government is on a path of continued collaboration with industry, but there's still a long way to go.[4]

Governments should start by clarifying how property rights over limited resources such as water on Mars, ice on the moon, or orbital slots (i.e., "parking spots" in space) will be governed. Recent steps—including NASA's offer to purchase lunar soil and rocks, the April 2020 executive order on the governance of space resources, and the 2015 Commercial Space Launch Competitiveness Act—indicate that the U.S. government is interested in establishing some form of regulatory framework to support the economic development of space.

In 2017, Luxembourg became the first European country to establish a legal framework securing private rights over resources mined in space, and similar steps have been taken at the domestic level in Japan and the United Arab Emirates. Moreover, nine countries (though Russia and China are notably missing) have signed the Artemis Accords, which lay out a vision for the sustainable, international development of the moon, Mars, and asteroids. These are important first steps, but they have yet to be clearly translated into comprehensive treaties that govern the fair use and allocation of scarce space resources among all major spacefaring nations.

In addition, governments should continue to fill the financial gaps in the still-maturing space-for-space economic ecosystem by funding basic scientific research in support of sending humans to space and by providing contracts to space startups. Similarly, while excessive regulation will stifle the industry, some government incentives, such as policies to reduce space debris, can help reduce the costs of operating in space for everyone in ways that would be difficult to coordinate independently.

3. Moving beyond geopolitical rivalries. Finally, the development of the space-for-space economy must not be undermined by earthly geopolitical rivalries, such as that between the United States and China. These conflicts will unavoidably extend into space at least to some extent, and military demand has long been an important source of funding for aerospace companies. But if not kept in check, such rivalries will not only distract attention and resources from borderless commercial pursuits but also create barriers and risks that hamper private investment.

On Earth, private economic activity has long tied together people whose states are at odds. The growing space-for-space economy offers exceptional potential to be such a force for unity—but it's the job of the world's governments not to get in the way. A collaborative, international approach to establishing—and enforcing—the rule of law in space will be essential to encouraging a healthy space-for-space economy.

. . .

Visions of a space-for-space economy have been around since the dawn of the Space Age, in the 1960s. Thus far, those hopes have gone largely unfulfilled—but this moment is different. For the first time in history, the private sector's capital, risk tolerance, and profit motive are being channeled into putting people in space. If we seize this opportunity, we will look back on this as the moment when we started the truly transformational project of building an economy and a society in space, for space.

TAKEAWAYS

Private companies are now sending humans into space, marking not only a tremendous technological achievement but also the first indication that an entirely new "space-for-space" industry is emerging—goods and services designed to supply space-bound customers.

✓ In the first stage of this burgeoning economy, private companies must sell to NASA and other government customers, since right now those organizations are the only source of in-space demand.

✓ Once we have private citizens in space, SpaceX and other companies will be poised to supply the demand they've created, creating a market that could dwarf the current government-led space industry—and eventually, the entire terrestrial economy as well.

NOTES

1. Matthew C. Weinzierl, Angela Acocella, and Mayuka Yamazaki, "Astroscale, Space Debris, and Earth's Orbital Commons," Harvard Business School, February 25, 2016, https://hbsp .harvard.edu/product/716037-PDF-ENG; and Matthew C. Weinzierl, Kylie Lucas, and Mehak Sarang, "SpaceX, Economies of Scale, and a Revolution in Space Access," Harvard Business School, April 9, 2020, https://hbsp.harvard.edu/product/720027-PDF-ENG.

2. William M. Brown and Herman Kahn, "Long-Term Prospects for Developments in Space: A Scenario Approach," NASA Technical Reports Server, October 30, 1977, https://ntrs.nasa.gov/citations /19780004167.

3. Matthew C. Weinzierl, "Space, the Final Economic Frontier," *Journal of Economic Perspectives* 32, no. 2 (Spring 2018), 173–192, https://www.hbs.edu/ris/Publication%20Files/jep.32.2.173 _Space,%20the%20Final%20Economic%20Frontier_413bf24d -42e6-4cea-8cc5-a0d2f6fc6a70.pdf.

4. Marcia Smith, "Space Council Gets Human Spaceflight Strategy Report," SpacePolicyOnline.com, November 19, 2018, https://spacepolicyonline.com/news/space-council-gets-human -spaceflight-strategy-report/.

Adapted from content posted on hbr.org, February 12, 2021 (product #H066NH).

Section 3

UPGRADING THE TECH INDUSTRY

8

WHAT'S NEXT FOR SILICON VALLEY?

by Maëlle Gavet

O ver the last 20 years, Silicon Valley has benefited from a once-in-a-lifetime alignment of advantages. American primacy, the ubiquity of cheap capital, the arrival of the smartphone (among other widely adopted tech innovations), and perhaps most significant, a benign regulatory environment have all conspired to create a historic concentration of wealth and power. The titans of the Valley and their heirs have been free to roam far ahead of lawmakers, watchdogs, and tax codes.

But that might not be true for much longer. Despite the fact that many public tech companies saw their valuations skyrocket during the lockdown and that the Covid-19 pandemic has accelerated mass adoption in e-commerce, online payments, telemedicine, and videoconferencing, there are signs that the gilded age for consumer internet businesses may be drawing to a close.

Four main driving forces are behind this.

First, the near-total dominance of the top tech giants—Facebook, Amazon, Alphabet (Google), Apple, and Microsoft—has become stifling. These companies not only hoover up top talent but they have grown to such a size and have expanded into adjacent markets to such an extent that they are suffocating all but the best new tech businesses. Smaller companies that compete in the markets that Big Tech considers strategic—an ever-expanding list—risk becoming targets of the full financial power of the giants, who aim to crush or buy possible contenders before they grow beyond a certain size. This hegemony impacts innovation and centralizes capital allocation.

Second, triggered in part by the poor post-IPO performances of Uber and Lyft—as well as by those of smaller companies like Casper, SmileDirectClub, Super League Gaming, and YayYo, and the WeWork/SoftBank debacle—investors, both private and institutional, are calibrating their approach. They are tightening requirements for additional financing to reflect the fact that a clear path to profitability, and not just exponential growth or "blitzscaling," is now considered key. This, combined with the pandemic hitting certain sectors especially hard, has exposed the suspect business models of some startups. In the absence of easy access to funding, whether because of the pandemic or because of precrisis problems, a number of them have seen their investors withdraw and have been forced to close.

Third, regulators, the media, and the public at large are now far more familiar with the downside of tech and the multiple ways the promises made to consumers have been broken. Mass privacy breaches, voter manipulation, disinformation, more-precarious working arrangements, life-threatening products, or the outlandish behavior of certain founders were largely tolerated until a few years ago, mainly because of public ignorance and faith in tech-bro mantras such as "Move fast and break things" and "We're making the world a better place." Today, the tech industry receives much more critical scrutiny as the cost of the industry's unfettered reach and toxic side effects becomes increasingly clear—think of how social media and personalized search results make us more skeptical of science and more hardened in our opinions, or how short-term rentals drive rent increases.

Fourth, similarly, the public mood has decidedly shifted, with more people believing that tech should be accountable for its impact on society. As the tech giants have reached market caps equivalent to midsize national economies, expectations and moral obligations have grown, too. As of this writing, Facebook has a market cap of more than $700 billion, up from $240 billion in just five years, while Apple, Amazon, Microsoft, and Alphabet are now trillion-dollar-plus companies. Even the Business Roundtable, America's most influential group of corporate bosses, has taken to cheerleading "capitalism with a conscience" with their 2019 statement on the purpose of a corporation asserting a "modern standard for corporate responsibility."[1]

All of these trends point to a reckoning on the horizon. Two months before the November 2020 presidential vote, according to Pew Research, 73% of Americans said they were not very confident or not at all confident in the ability of tech giants like Facebook, Twitter, and Google to prevent the misuse of their platforms to influence the election.[2] Separate research found that 85% of respondents felt Big Tech has too much power.[3] Meanwhile, there's a growing expectation on both sides of the Atlantic for tech companies to pay their taxes fairly and in full, rather than play the tax-minimization game they've gotten away with for so long; researchers at Fair Tax Mark, a U.K. nonprofit that campaigns for tax transparency and justice, identified a gap of $155.3 billion between the expected rate of tax and the cash taxes actually paid by Facebook, Amazon, Netflix, Google, Apple, and Microsoft (collectively known as FANGAM) between 2010 and 2019.[4]

Against this backdrop, it's clear that the typical tech business templates of the past few decades will no longer cut it—from either a business or societal perspective—for companies who plan to be around, let alone thrive, 20 years from now. The ready availability of investor cash coupled with sky-high revenue-growth expectations, which together incentivize predatory pricing (undercutting competitors by using venture capital billions to keep prices of, say, an Uber ride or a DoorDash delivery artificially low); the exploitation of independent contractors in the on-demand economy; the algorithms designed to fuel outrage, which increases time spent on social media platforms; the advertising optimization that encourages privacy-shredding microtargeting—these practices are all under threat and unsustainable.

What, then, will the tech business models of the future look like? Given the changing conditions outlined above, thriving in the next era of tech will likely involve meeting a different set of goals. While it is something of a taboo in the Valley (and on Sand Hill Road in particular) to say so, tech's new era will very likely see slower yet more sustainable growth and reduced profitability.

All these changes in funding, regulation, and public sentiment will likely alter key aspects of the current scale-first business models I've described—and will disrupt existing sources of revenue. Based on my 15 years working in tech as an executive for large tech companies and a consultant for the Boston Consulting Group, and now 18 months writing a book about how to make Big Tech more empathetic and human-centric, I believe we're about to see some major shifts in this rapidly evolving environment—and that there may be new opportunities for a different kind of tech company:

- **The microtargeted advertising model will increasingly come under attack and will weaken:** Due to growing concerns around privacy invasion, the dissemination of conspiracy theories, and voter manipulation, look for companies to move away from the microtargeting approach used by Twitter, Facebook, and Google/YouTube. The value of this model has been contested, and scandals related to hate speech, privacy violations, data breaches, and more have flourished. Web-based advertising platforms will likely limit microtargeting to a very narrow subset of categories and advertisers while moving toward some kind of "freemium" model more acceptable to regulators and users.

- **Look for more rights for gig workers and the end of "zero hours" contracts:** Changing attitudes and user and customer pressure will likely force disruptors of physical consumer businesses, such as Uber, Lyft, Airbnb, and DoorDash, to offer protections to full-time equivalent workers. Ultimately, this will make these companies somewhat smaller and less profitable than the FANGAM-style tech giants their investors envisioned, possibly making this model less attractive to VCs seeking outsize returns. But new companies in this space, freed from the endless brunch of venture-cash, have an opportunity to become genuinely profitable and sustainable from the get-go.

- **There will be big winners and many failures in the direct-to-consumer (D2C) and online product subscription models:** Over the past decade there has been much buzz around online D2C businesses for physical goods, such as Dollar Shave Club, Harry's, The Honest Company, and Casper. In theory, by cutting out the middleman (that is, the retailer), D2C companies can sell their products at lower price points than legacy brands and double down on product. But it turns out that D2C isn't all it was cracked up to be. It's not that the model is unviable, per se; it's just that most D2C businesses haven't really built any domain expertise: Their products aren't necessarily better, they haven't mastered digital marketing, and their unit economics are less attractive than at first glance, because of acquisition costs and lack of scale. There are also too many of them, which is why only the biggest and best-run D2C companies will win and many will fail. Yet out of these ashes, new business opportunities will arise. As consumer demand continues to shift online, I believe we will see a new generation of platform infrastructure businesses that will help any consumer brand become a D2C player. These platform infrastructure businesses (e.g., Stripe and Shopify) will benefit from the aggregation they create—you can't be a master of digital marketing with one small D2C brand, but you can with 100. This trend will also power legacy brands to transition faster to D2C.

- **Companies that focus on "conscious capitalism" and empathetic tech will have an advantage:** In an era when consumers demand higher ethical standards from all brands, the leading tech companies will increasingly be expected to exercise their power with far greater responsibility and will be held accountable by regulators, users, boards, investors, and even their own staff (something we're seeing more and more of) to make the right trade-offs. These decisions include: 1) whether to benefit from high user engagement stemming from outrage and right-wing populism on platforms, or to provide a universal communication platform free from disinformation, bullying, and hate through stricter standards (e.g., Twitter, Facebook, YouTube); 2) whether to offer consumers lower prices with less vetting, or to limit inventory by cracking down on bogus or potentially dangerous products or situations (e.g., Amazon, Airbnb); and 3) how to support the legitimate security efforts of democratic governments without enabling surveillance, profiling, and government overreach (e.g., Google, Microsoft, Apple). The list goes on. While I'm not suggesting that all startup founders and legacy CEOs should turn to social entrepreneurship and build B Corps, research shows that creating value-based and empathy-driven companies makes business sense: A study of exceptionally purpose-conscious firms demonstrated that they outperformed the S&P 500 index by a factor of 10.5 between 1996 and 2011.

The convergence of these trends means some businesses will be significantly downsized or will even disappear altogether—but others will thrive, albeit with different business models and economics along with reduced expectations and growth trajectories. Still, there is a wild card in all this: the regulators. As businesses are pushed toward monopoly and aggregation to achieve the profitability and competitive advantage required by the markets, increasingly hawkish regulators will likely turn toward antitrust and hands-on oversight and interventions—and the big question is how far they might go. The uncertainty around future regulators' actions on both sides of the Atlantic is particularly high, given how the looming economic crisis renders protectionism and the defense of national champions more and more tempting. My hope is that the combination of industry-led initiatives, increased consumer scrutiny, and balanced regulation will help tech return to its original aspirations of being a force for good and progress for humanity.

Interestingly, this shifting landscape creates, in my view, a unique opportunity for legacy businesses—not just to pivot digitally but to become the Platforms 3.0. Legacy businesses have huge advantages: They know how to operate in the physical world, they have marketing teams who know how to build and sustain brands, and crucially, they know how to operate profitably in multiple territories within the law. It won't be easy—most will fail—but the ones that succeed will be richly rewarded.

TAKEAWAYS

There are signs that the gilded age of tech giants may be drawing to a close. Change is coming to Silicon Valley.

✓ Four main trends suggest the environment that allowed companies such as Facebook, Twitter, and Google to flourish might not exist for much longer: the stifling dominance of these top companies; changing investor attitudes; increased scrutiny from regulators, the media, and the public; and a growing emphasis on ethical capitalism.

✓ As a result, the tech industry will likely experience major shifts, including the decline of micro-targeted advertising, more rights for gig workers, a sorting of direct-to-consumer startups into big winners and many failures, and a pivot to "conscious capitalism."

✓ The grand result will be slower but more sustainable growth throughout the industry.

NOTES

1. "Business Roundtable Redefines the Purpose of a Corporation to Promote 'An Economy That Serves All Americans,'" businessroundtable.org, August 19, 2019, https://www.businessroundtable.org/business-roundtable-redefines-the-purpose-of-a-corporation-to-promote-an-economy-that-serves-all-americans.

2. Ted Van Green, "Few Americans Are Confident in Tech Companies to Prevent Misuse of Their Platforms in the 2020 Election," FactTank, pewresearch.org, September 9, 2020, https://www.pewresearch.org/fact-tank/2020/09/09/few-americans-are-confident-in-tech-companies-to-prevent-misuse-of-their-platforms-in-the-2020-election/.

3. "New Polling Highlights America's Views on Big Tech, Facebook Boycott, Mark Zuckerberg," accountabletech.org, July 23, 2020, https://accountabletech.org/media/polling/.

4. Vijay Govindarajan, Anup Srivastava, Hussein Warsame, and Luminita Enache, "Tech Giants, Taxes, and a Looming Global Trade War," hbr.org, August 24, 2020, https://hbr.org/2020/08/tech-giants-taxes-and-a-looming-global-trade-war; and "Tax Gap of Silicon Six over $100 Billion This Decade," fairtaxmark.net, December 2, 2019, https://fairtaxmark.net/tax-gap-of-silicon-six-over-100-billion-so-far-this-decade/.

Adapted from content posted on hbr.org, September 30, 2020 (product #H05WC5).

9

WHAT IT'S LIKE TO BE A BLACK MAN IN TECH

by LeRon L. Barton

A s a Black man who has worked in the technology sector for more than 20 years, I can tell you that my race has almost always been a factor in how I am viewed and treated. In many of the companies I have worked for, if not in all of them, I have been one of, and sometimes the sole, African American in my department.

When you're the only Black person in an office, you notice it.

Glancing around, you notice that no one looks like you, talks like you, or has a story like yours. Nobody has the gall to approach you and say, "Hey, out of the 40 people on this floor, you're the only Black guy." But you sense that everyone else notices it too.

You sense it from the stares you receive when you walk through the door, from the looks on people's faces when they learn that you're competent at your job, from the alienation you feel after not being invited to lunch with your peers, and from the awkwardness they project when they try to engage you in everyday conversation.

Being Black in tech, like being Black in America, is an exercise of mental toughness. Your mind is constantly wondering, "How long can I last?"

The underrepresentation of African Americans in tech has been an issue since the 1970s, when the Bay Area became known as "Silicon Valley." Frederick Terman, former Stanford University dean of engineering, had been encouraging his students to start their own companies since the 1950s. The Bay Area ultimately became home to Hewlett-Packard, Intel, and later Facebook, Apple, and Google. Though the lack of diversity at these companies has been questioned and criticized for decades, the problem hasn't seen much resolution.

In 2018, according to Silicon Valley Bank, only 1% of venture capital dollars went to Black startup founders and Black employees made up only 2.8% of Google's technical roles and 4.8% of their entire workforce.[1] More recently, Twitter reported that Black employees made up only 6% of their staff and Facebook reported 3.8% of their employees were Black.[2] All of this contributes to an environment that continues to be hostile toward African Americans, one that tells us, "You are not welcome."

Over the years, I have talked to many Black folks who also work in tech, from technical support representatives and system engineers to network architects and programmers. We have swapped stories that would make your jaw drop: stories about having the validity of our work badges questioned by the companies that employ us, stories of white team members who perceive us as the "diversity hire" and are surprised that our educations were not paid for by sports scholarships, and stories of peers who are shocked that we didn't come from broken homes or that we can speak correct English. The number of times we have heard, "You are so articulate," when answering a question or speaking up at a meeting is mind-blowing.

All of these stories, along with the unending microaggressions—the mispronouncing of names, the questions about where we are *really* from, and the awe at the fact that we can fulfill and succeed at the jobs we were hired to do: It wears on us—on me—mentally.

To create real change, much work still needs to be done at the organizational and leadership levels. At the same time, Black people cannot afford to wait around for this change to happen. We deserve to take up space, move up, and thrive in Big Tech—and we should, even as we continue to fight for more diverse, equitable, and inclusive workspaces.

If you are Black and you are interested in or currently entering the tech industry, know that it is not going to be easy. You are a minority in a sector that is incredibly slow in addressing race and diversity. But also know that you can find comfort and learn from people who look like you and who share your experience. I've spent more than two decades navigating this space, and I can be one of those people. I can offer you some advice.

Below are three lessons I have learned as an IT professional. These points are not meant to solve racism at work or convince tech companies to hire more African Americans. They are meant to provide you with skills you can use to navigate this industry, set healthy boundaries, and protect your mental health and your career development as you grow.

The most powerful thing you can do is be yourself.

The first piece of advice I can offer any Black person entering a predominately white tech company is: Don't change yourself to fit in. Many times, as one of the few African Americans in a firm, I downplayed who I was and how I felt. I would code-switch, ignore microaggressions, and bypass things that were not professional. Why? Because I wanted to fit in. I didn't want to be excluded or make waves, and I feared that if I did, I might be fired.

But there were consequences to this. My coworkers felt comfortable making racist jokes around me. "I hear police sirens—they must be coming to arrest LeRon," got a lot of laughs. These kinds of comments about Black people were said often, and just as often they went unchallenged. I felt the constant stress of "wearing two masks," one for work and the other for my life. I understood what W. E. B. Du Bois meant when he wrote about "double consciousness," living as a Black man through the eyes of society and himself.

It took 10 years for me to grow tired of "shrinking myself" at work. I started to speak up for myself, and for others. I brought attention to discussions that could be considered inflammatory by confronting the people who initiated them. I escalated these issues to management. Unfortunately, there were consequences to this too.

When I became more outspoken about race—about how few Black folk are employed in tech and how we are treated—I became known as "that Black guy." There were certain discussions and panels I was not privy or invited to, opportunities I was not presented with, and possibly even promotions that I did not receive. But I was more

OK with those consequences than the ones born out of my silence.

There is a saying, "I would rather be rejected for who I am than accepted for who I am not." When you are true to yourself and honest with who you are and where you are, that is a powerful thing. In my experience, when you stop trying to be the nonconfrontational Black person and call out the inequalities you see, a weight will be lifted from your shoulders. You will carry a new weight—the weight of being your authentic self in a space that may feel threatened by that. But this is the first step toward your personal growth, toward figuring out what you value and who you want to be at work, and maybe, one day, toward a larger systemic change.

The second most powerful thing you can do is speak up.

Being the only Black person on your team often means that other people begin to view you as the designated "Black expert." Whenever the questions come up, "Do Black people like this?" or "Why do Black people do that?" you will be approached first.

In my experience, these questions are annoying but often innocuous. But the mood changes when there is a police shooting of an unarmed Black man or when yet another video of a white woman accusing a Black man of stealing or trespassing goes viral. Interactions, even casual ones, become more tense. In moments like these I've come to realize that in my teammates' eyes, I represent all Black people—regardless of age, sociological background, nationality, or other factors.

Confrontation is never easy, but my advice here is to be up front the first time something like this ever happens to you—and it probably will. By letting people know immediately when their comments or questions are offensive, they will grow more aware of how inappropriate their behavior is.

The first time someone approaches you with a question you aren't comfortable answering, let them know that you are not the authority of all things Black. Explain that we are not a monolithic group but people who have all lived different experiences. If someone jokes and asks, "Hey, do all Black people . . . ?" I would respond in a firm but assertive way, "I don't know all Black people, so I wouldn't know how to answer that. Your question is offensive."

If you are not comfortable confronting the person in the moment, schedule time to talk to them privately and let them know why their comment was hurtful. Either way, speak up and let your teammates know how you feel. Set the precedent that those questions are unacceptable.

Finally, know when to ask for help.

Whenever I give a talk at a corporation, I emphasize: "If someone files a complaint about racism, it is everyone's responsibility to address it." Once it happens, everyone needs to stop, direct their attention toward the incident, and listen.

One of the biggest failings I've seen in tech management is the lack of ownership. If you tell your manager that you have experienced discrimination, that you feel the work environment is hostile, or that you have seen an act of racism, know that your concerns are *always* valid and they deserve to be taken seriously.

Sadly, in my experience, these complaints are almost never taken seriously and there is very little, if any, discipline issued to the offending party. The first instinct of most supervisors and managers I have dealt with is to put the blame on the person being discriminated against, tell them they need to learn how to take a "joke," or explain away the racist incident as an example of "cultural insensitivity."

When this happens, you, the Black employee, will not feel heard. You may feel gaslighted or think, "Maybe the problem is me? Maybe I don't fit in here? Maybe I need to change?"

Let me answer those questions for you: No, you are not the problem. You may not always fit in, but that doesn't mean you need to change. This is not an employee issue or a departmental issue, it is an organizational issue—and your organization needs to be held accountable.

If management is not addressing your report of discrimination and racism, escalate it. Schedule time with your manager's manager and explain why you are raising the issue to them. If that person does not address it properly, go to *their* manager. Do not be afraid to continue to escalate the issue. At the highest level you would report it to Human Resources.

To present the strongest case possible, provide documentation. Write down every incident you or your colleagues experience, including the times and dates of each occurrence, what was said or done, and who was involved. If you have allies who can back your statements and support you, even better. It's harder to ignore a group of people than it is to ignore just one person.

Sometimes you may have to decide if you truly can be who you are at your company. If you have to compromise yourself and your morals to stay, then it is not the right place for you. And it is OK to choose to leave.

In times of fear or doubt, do as I do, and think about this quote from Zora Neale Hurston: "If you are silent about your pain, they'll kill you and say you enjoyed it."

As a Black employee in tech, tell your truth. Talk about your experience. Do not water down what you have faced as one of the few in the field. When I started to be more outspoken and follow the advice that I'm giving you, I realized that I am not an individual but part of a collective. My efforts to make tech more equitable are not just about me but also about the networking engineer, the programmer, the project manager, and all of the other professionals that will come after—and that includes you.

TAKEAWAYS

The underrepresentation of Black people in tech has been an issue since the emergence of Silicon Valley. There is scarce venture capital for Black-owned startups, and the percentage of Black employees at tech firms is low. Microaggressions and noninclusive cultures are the norm.

✓ Much work still needs to be done at the organizational and leadership levels to create real change, but we cannot afford to wait around for this change to take place. Black people deserve to take up space, move up, and thrive in the tech industry, now.

✓ If you are Black and you are interested in or currently entering the tech industry, know that it is not going to be easy. But also know that you can find comfort and learn from people who look like you and who share your experiences.

✓ Black people should consider three pieces of advice when entering the tech industry: Be yourself, speak up, and know when to ask for help.

NOTES

1. Nitasha Tiku, "Black Tech Founders Say Venture Capital Needs to Move Past 'Diversity Theater,'" *Washington Post*, June 10, 2020, https://www.washingtonpost.com/technology/2020/06/10/racial -gap-vc-firms/; and Nick Bastone, "Google Employees Are Circulating a Memo Written by a Former Googler Who Says They Encountered Racism and 'Never Stopped Feeling the Burden of Being Black' While Working There," businessinsider.com, August 15, 2019, https://www.businessinsider.com/black-former-google -employee-writes-memo-about-racism-at-company-2019-8.

2. Justin Philips, "Does Twitter Love the Idea of Black Employees as Much as It Loves Black Twitter?" *San Francisco Chronicle*, July 15, 2020, https://www.sfchronicle.com/living/article/does -Twitter-love-the-idea-of-Black-employees-as-15410658.php; and Alison Durkee, "Black Employees Allege Racial Discrimination

at Facebook in New Legal Complaint," forbes.com, July 2, 2020, https://www.forbes.com/sites/alisondurkee/2020/07/02/black -employees-allege-racial-discrimination-at-facebook-in-new-legal -complaint/?sh=68ff534f426d.

Adapted from content posted on hbr.org, March 4, 2021.

SOCIAL MEDIA COMPANIES SHOULD SELF-REGULATE. NOW.

by Michael A. Cusumano, Annabelle Gawer,
and David B. Yoffie

The world witnessed the worst example of the impact that digital platforms can have on society with the debacle at the U.S. Capitol on January 6, 2021. Not only did supporters of Donald Trump try to disrupt the certification of the Electoral College votes, but this deplorable incident was, in large part, fomented over social media.

In the past, Twitter and Facebook have been reluctant to censor posts about conspiracy theories and fake news.

Digital platforms also have benefited from a 1996 law, Section 230 of the Communications Decency Act, that grants them immunity from liabilities related to third-party-hosted content. Nevertheless, prompted by false accusations of rigged elections and other fake news, the leading digital platforms in social media recently began tagging some posts as unreliable or untrue and removing some videos. Following the January 6 insurrection attempt, Twitter and Facebook also banned Trump from using their platforms because promotion of violence and criminal acts violates their terms of service. For similar reasons, Apple and Google removed the alternative social media platform Parler from their app stores and Amazon stopped hosting the service.

How did we get into this mess?

Digital platforms can be highly profitable businesses that connect users and other market actors in ways not possible before the internet. When they are successful, they generate powerful feedback loops called "network effects" and then monetize them by selling advertisements. But what happened at the U.S. Capitol illustrates how digital platforms can be double-edged swords. Yes, they have generated trillions of dollars in wealth. But they have also enabled the distribution of fake news and fake products, manipulation of digital content for political purposes, and promotion of dangerous misinformation on elections, vaccines, and other public health matters.

The social dilemma is clear: Digital platforms can be used for evil as well as good.

What's the solution? Should platform companies wait for governments to impose potentially intrusive controls and respond defensively? Or should they act preemptively?

Governments will inevitably get more engaged in oversight. However, we believe that platforms should become more aggressive at self-regulation *now*. To explore the feasibility of self-regulation, we researched the history of self-regulation before and after the widespread adoption of the internet. We found that companies have often risked creating a "tragedy of the commons" when they put their short-term, individual self-interests ahead of the good of the consuming public or the industry overall, and, in the long term, destroy the environment that made them successful in the first place.

Before the internet era, several industries, such as movies, video games, broadcasting content, television advertising, and computerized airline reservation systems, faced similar issues and managed to self-regulate with some success. At the same time, these historical examples suggest that self-regulation worked best when there were credible threats of government regulation. The bottom line: Self-regulation may be the key to avoiding a potential tragedy-of-the-commons scenario for digital platforms.

What is "self-regulation"? This refers to the steps companies or industry associations take to preempt or supplement governmental rules and guidelines. For an individual company, self-regulation ranges from self-monitoring for regulatory violations to proactive "corporate social responsibility" (CSR) initiatives. Leaving it up to companies to monitor and restrain themselves can sometimes devolve into a self-regulatory or regulatory "charade." But that doesn't need to be the case.

For many decades, companies in the business of producing movies, video games, and television shows and commercials all faced issues around the appropriateness of "content" in a way that resembles today's social media platforms. To keep regulators at bay, the movie and video game industries resorted to a self-imposed and self-monitored rating system, still in operation today. The broadcasting and advertisement sectors in the 1950s and 1960s faced pushback on the appropriateness of advertisements, with issues resembling what we see today in online advertising. Launched in 1960, the airline reservation industry, led by American Airlines' Sabre system, introduced self-preferencing in search results, similar to complaints made against Google and Amazon. Self-regulation in these cases often delivered effective and inexpensive guidelines for company operations as well as forestalled more-intrusive government intervention.

History provides several lessons for today's digital platforms.

First, our leading technology companies need to anticipate when government regulation is likely to become a key factor in their businesses. In movies, radio and television broadcasting, airline reservations via computers, and other new industries, there often occurs a vacuum in regulation in the early years. Then, after a kind of "Wild West" environment, governments step in to regulate or pressure firms to curb abuses. To avoid problematic government regulation, platform companies need to introduce their own controls on behavior and usage before the government revokes all Section 230 protections, a notion that has been debated in Congress. Technology that exploits big data, artificial intelligence, and machine learning, with some human editing, will increasingly give digital platforms the ability to curate what happens on their platforms. The issue is really to what extent the big platforms have the will to self-regulate. The decisions by Facebook, Twitter, Amazon, Apple, and Google during the first week in January 2021 were steps in the right direction.

Second, we find that firms in new industries tend to eschew self-regulation when the perceived costs imply a significant reduction in revenues or profits. Managers rarely like industry regulations that appear "bad for business." However, this strategy can be self-defeating. If bad behavior undermines consumer trust, then digital platforms will not continue to thrive. Look closely at Section 230. It states that "no provider or user of an interactive computer service shall be treated as the publisher or speaker of any information provided by another information content provider." This act gives online intermediaries broad immunity from liability for user-generated content posted on their sites. Executives and company lawyers should feel comfortable making reasonable curation decisions under Section 230. However, they have generally resisted and argued that their legal and political positions would be more secure if they avoided potentially controversial curation. Internal debates ranging from free speech versus censorship to how much curation the firm can perform before it crosses the line from platform to "publisher" have led most social media companies to resist aggressive curation until recent years. However, Section 230 also includes a "good Samaritan" exception. This allows platforms to remove or moderate content deemed obscene or offensive, as long as it is done in good faith. There have been growing calls from both Democrats and Republicans to repeal Section 230 because of accusations of bias (i.e., not acting in good faith) and very little curation over the past decade by Twitter, Facebook/Instagram, and other platforms. More explicit and transparent self-regulation, like we observed after the U.S. Capitol debacle, might well produce a better outcome for social media platforms, at least compared to leaving their fate up to Congress.

Third, proactive self-regulation has often been more successful when coalitions of firms in the same sector worked together. We saw this coalition-type activity in movie and video-game rating systems limiting violent, profane, or sexual content; television advertisement rules curbing the promotion of unhealthy products like alcohol and tobacco; and computerized online airline reservations giving equal treatment to airlines, without favoring the system owners. Similarly, social media companies implemented codes of conduct on terrorist activity. Since individual firms may hesitate to enact self-regulation if they incur added costs that their competitors do not, industry coalitions have the benefit of reducing free riding. Now is the ideal time for more "coopetition," where platforms compete as well as cooperate with rivals.

Fourth, we find that firms or industry coalitions get serious about self-regulation primarily when they see a credible threat of government regulation, even if it may hurt short-term sales and profits. This pattern occurred with tobacco and cigarette ads, airline reservations, social media ads for terrorist group recruitment, and pornographic material. That threat should be clear and obvious to digital platforms now.

In sum, history suggests that modern digital platforms should not wait for governments to impose controls; they should act decisively and proactively now. While the costs of government action in the internet era have been modest so far, the regulatory environment is changing fast. Given the increasing likelihood of government action, the goal of self-regulation should be to avoid a tragedy of the commons, where a lack of trust destroys the environment that has allowed digital platforms to thrive. Going forward, governments and digital platforms will also need to work together more closely. Since more government oversight of Twitter, Facebook, Google, Amazon, and other platforms seems inevitable, new institutional mechanisms for more-participative forms of regulation may be critical to their long-term survival and success.

TAKEAWAYS

Tech companies face the real threat of government intervention in response to socially harmful content they are publishing. To avoid heavy regulation, tech companies should form an industry coalition and act decisively and proactively to self-regulate now.

✓ When companies put individual self-interest ahead of the good of the consuming public or the industry overall, in the long term they destroy the environment that made them successful in the first place.

✓ Industries including the movie, television advertising, and video game sectors self-regulated in ways that benefited society while keeping government regulators at bay.

✓ Proactive self-regulation is often more successful when coalitions of firms in the same sector work together. Now is the ideal time for more "coopetition," where platforms compete as well as cooperate with rivals.

Adapted from content posted on hbr.org, January 15, 2021 (product #H064SP).

HOW GREEN IS YOUR SOFTWARE?

by Sanjay Podder, Adam Burden,
Shalabh Kumar Singh, and Regina Maruca

Without doubt, software is the backbone of virtually all the intelligent solutions designed to support the environment. It's critical, for example, in efforts to tackle deforestation and reduce emissions. In many instances, however, software is also part and parcel of a rapidly growing carbon footprint. In fact, recent and proliferating digital technologies have begun to worsen many of the environmental problems they are aimed at solving. But companies can make software an integral part of their sustainability efforts by accounting for its carbon footprint in its design, development, and deployment and by rethinking some aspects of how the data centers that provide cloud-based services operate.

Let's be clear: On its own, software doesn't consume energy or emit any harmful discharge. The problem lies in the way software is developed for use—and then in the way it is used. Software runs on hardware, and as the former continues to grow, so does reliance on the machines to make it run.

For example, blockchain drives some of the most advanced green solutions available, such as microgrids that allow residents to trade environmentally friendly energy. This software innovation is also behind the development of cryptocurrency. In 2019, researchers at the University of Cambridge estimated that the energy needed to maintain the Bitcoin network surpassed that of the entire nation of Switzerland.[1]

Then there's the information and communications technology sector as whole. By 2040, it is expected to account for 14% of the world's carbon footprint—up from about 1.5% in 2007.[2]

The very development of software can be energy intensive. For example, consider what we learned when we trained an artificial intelligence (AI) model on a small, publicly available data set of iris flowers. The AI model achieved accuracy of 96.17% in classifying the flowers' different species with only 964 joules of energy.[3] The next

1.74%-point increase in accuracy required 2,815 joules of energy consumption. The last 0.08% incremental increase in accuracy took nearly 400% more energy than the first stage.

Now consider that same example in the context of the bigger picture of AI overall. Training a single-neural-network model today can emit as much carbon as five cars in their lifetimes.[4] And the amount of computational power required to run large AI training models has been increasing exponentially, with a 3.4-month doubling time.[5]

All that said, it wouldn't make sense to limit reliance on software as a means to enable work, especially in the post-Covid world, where working from home or remote locations could become the norm for many. Nor would limiting software-driven innovation be a viable response.

However, companies can make software an integral part of their sustainability efforts by judging its performance on its energy efficiency as much as on traditional parameters (e.g., functionality, security, scalability, and accessibility) and by including green practices and targets as criteria for CIO performance reviews.

Ultimately, the rewards would outweigh the challenges: The early, increased scrutiny that building green software requires translates into a higher-quality product: leaner, cleaner, and more fit for its purpose. These qualities also offset additional up-front costs. Green software will help large companies meet their environmental, social, and corporate governance (ESG) targets, an increasingly important performance measure for stakeholders. Finally, our research (soon to be published) has shown that newly minted computer engineers are increasingly weighing a company's focus on sustainability when choosing an employer; a commitment to green software can be a persuasive draw.

So how can companies go green with their software? It's a three-part process that begins with articulating a strategy that sets some boundaries, then targets the software development life cycle, and makes the cloud green as well. No single company that we know of is engaged fully in this process as we describe it and reaping the full benefits of purposefully green software. However, a growing number of businesses—including Google, Volkswagen, and Rainforest (itself a software testing company)—are deploying a variety of the following approaches and techniques.

Articulate a strategy that guides trade-offs and allows for flexibility.

Doing this will get IT teams thinking about the right level of tolerance for their software's environmental effects. There are almost always trade-offs between business and environmental goals, and software engineers need to be able to determine where the go/no-go line is. Think back to the AI model we trained on the iris flower data set. Whether that last step to increase the accuracy is worth the energy it consumes is a business decision that requires clear guidance from the top.

It is equally important that the strategy call for flexibility—allowing engineers running room to improvise and to learn through trial and error. Green software is still an emerging field, largely limited to academia. There are no guidebooks for engineers in this area.

Finally, this broad strategy should suggest the metrics needed to measure progress. For software updates, these would not be difficult to set (for example, by determining how much more energy a new version consumes than the previous version). For new software, however, useful measures would be more difficult to define. Initially they could include such measures as memory-use efficiencies, the amount of data used, and floating-point (mathematical) operations per second.

Review and refine the software development life cycle.

Start by asking: What is the smallest possible environmental footprint we could make with this application?

Use that expectation to guide the first stages of the software development cycle. This expectation may shift as you gain knowledge, but it can be a great help in informing the feasibility study and any assessment of trade-offs between alternate approaches.

Then develop recommendations on, for example, the algorithms, programming languages, application programming interfaces (APIs), and libraries you can draw on to minimize carbon emissions. And demand constant assessment of alternatives that might be more efficient. These assessments would test the software's compatibility across various energy-constrained hardware designs, such as mobile, car, and home controls.

At the deployment stage, monitor real-time power consumption through techniques such as dynamic code analysis. The data you gather will be critical for understanding the gaps between the design choices and actual energy profiles.

Some companies are offering tools to help develop power-aware and increasingly efficient systems. For example, Intel offers developers tools and resources for managing energy consumption. The company's Software Development Assistant allows engineers to take energy measurements from the system as it executes specific workloads within their application and determine its efficiency.

However, these sorts of tools are in short supply. Assessing key trade-offs between carbon emissions and business objectives such as flexibility is still an uphill climb.

Make the cloud green.

Modern applications are almost always deployed in the cloud. But the exponential growth in cloud-based services has resulted in the rapid expansion of power-intensive data centers. Data centers consume about 2% of global electricity today; by 2030, they could consume as much as 8%.[6]

To date, most efforts to make data centers green have focused on optimizing hardware (by reducing the incidence of overheated servers) and reducing carbon emissions (by increasing the mix of renewable energy that powers them). These techniques are helping to address the problem; however, including sustainable software interventions opens new opportunities to save energy.

For example, eliminating duplicate copies of data or compressing data into smaller chunks would save energy. So would deploying graphics-processing units to manage workloads at the edge (near the device or the end user), which creates efficiencies by breaking up large tasks into smaller ones and divvying them up among many processors.

Adopting greener server architectures will likely prove crucial for saving energy consumption. Using virtual servers, for example, would help companies scale up their servers on demand, conserving energy in enterprise data centers. Virtualization essentially enables the creation of multiple simulated environments (or dedicated resources) from a single, physical hardware system. Containerization, essentially an improvement over virtual systems, is another option. Where serverless computing separates applications at the hardware level, containerization separates them at the operating-system level.

Newer application architectures—such as serverless computing or functions-as-a-service (FaaS)—enable even more control over capacity and by extension, energy consumption. Serverless computing, for example, efficiently shares infrastructure resources by executing functions only on demand. And since it bills by execution time, it compels programmers to improve their codes' efficiency. Large serverless-computing service providers such as AWS Lambda and Microsoft Functions, for example, provide for continuous scaling with a pay-as-you-use cost model.

Whether it is the mobile phone that requires more-efficient use of resources and computing power to save energy or the cloud data center where servers must be optimized for energy consumption, the need for green software will continue to grow. By including software in your sustainability efforts now, your company will have a head start in this important area.

The authors thank Vikrant Kaulgud and Vibhu Saujanya Sharma from Accenture Labs and Shruti Shalini and Dave Light from Accenture Research for their contributions to this article.

TAKEAWAYS

The way software is designed, developed, and deployed can have a major impact on energy consumption. Including software in your sustainability efforts calls for a three-part process:

✓ Articulate a strategy that guides trade-offs and allows for flexibility. Doing so will get teams thinking about the right level of tolerance and the right metrics to measure progress and allow engineers room to experiment.

✓ Review and refine the software development life cycle. Set environmental footprint targets early in the cycle; develop recommendations on algorithms, programming languages, and APIs to minimize carbon emissions; and leverage tools that monitor real-time power consumption.

✓ Make the cloud green. Consider software solutions including data deduplication and compression, as well as greener server architectures such as virtualization, containerization, and functions-as-a-service.

NOTES

1. James Vincent, "Bitcoin Consumes More Energy Than Switzerland, According to New Estimate," *The Verge*, July 4, 2019, https://www.theverge.com/2019/7/4/20682109/bitcoin-energy -consumption-annual-calculation-cambridge-index-cbeci-country -comparison.

2. Pam Wright, "Your Smartphone Has a Dark Side That May Surprise You," weather.com, March 29, 2018, https://weather.com /science/environment/news/2018-03-28-smartphones-danger -killing-planet.

3. Yong Cui, "The Iris Dataset—A Little Bit of History and Biology," towardsdatascience.com, April 25, 2020, https:// towardsdatascience.com/the-iris-dataset-a-little-bit-of-history-and -biology-fb4812f5a7b5.

4. Karen Hao, "Training a Single AI Model Can Emit as Much Carbon as Five Cars in Their Lifetimes," *MIT Technology Review*, June 6, 2019, https://www.technologyreview.com/2019/06/06

/239031/training-a-single-ai-model-can-emit-as-much-carbon-as
-five-cars-in-their-lifetimes/.

5. "AI and Compute," OpenAI.com, May 16, 2018, https://openai
.com/blog/ai-and-compute/.

6. Naomi Xu Elegant, "The Internet Cloud Has a Dirty Secret,"
fortune.com, September 18, 2019, https://fortune.com/2019/09
/18/internet-cloud-server-data-center-energy-consumption
-renewable-coal/.

Adapted from content posted on hbr.org, September 18, 2020 (product #H05V47).

About the Contributors

LeRON L. BARTON is a writer, author, and speaker based in San Francisco. He has written essays about race, mass incarceration, politics, tech, and dating. His writing has appeared in *Salon*, *Black Enterprise*, YourTango, The Good Men Project, *MEL Magazine*, TEDxWilsonPark, and Al Jazeera.

REID BLACKMAN is the founder and CEO of Virtue, an ethical risk consultancy that works with companies to integrate ethics and ethical risk mitigation into company culture and the development, deployment, and procurement of emerging technology products. He is also a senior adviser to Ernst & Young and sits on their Artificial Intelligence Advisory Board, and he is a member of the IEEE Ethically Aligned Design initiative. Prior to founding Virtue, Reid was a professor of philosophy at Colgate University and the University of North Carolina, Chapel Hill.

JAN B. BRÖNNEKE is the Director of Law and Economic Health Technologies at Germany's health innovation hub, where he advises the Federal Ministry of Health on the digital transformation of Germany's health-care system. Previously, he worked at the Federal Joint Committee, the highest decision-making body of the joint self-government of Germany's health-care system, and as a manager of a health-care law firm.

ADAM BURDEN is Accenture's Chief Software Engineer and leads the Intelligent Software Engineering Services practice. Follow him on Twitter @adampburden.

MICHAEL A. CUSUMANO is the Sloan Management Review Distinguished Professor of Management at the MIT Sloan School of Management. He is a coauthor of *The Business of Platforms: Strategy in the Age of Digital Competition, Innovation, and Power* (2019).

JÖRG F. DEBATIN is the Chairman of Germany's health innovation hub, where he advises the Federal Ministry of Health on the digital transformation of Germany's health-care system. Trained as a diagnostic radiologist, he previously served as the Medical Director and CEO of the University Medical Center Hamburg-Eppendorf and as Chief Technology and Medical Officer of GE Healthcare.

LARRY DOWNES is a coauthor of *Pivot to the Future: Discovering Value and Creating Growth in a Disrupted World*. His earlier books include *Big Bang Disruption, The Laws of Disruption,* and *Unleashing the Killer App.*

ABHINAV GAIHA is a product manager at Google.

VISHAL GAUR is the Emerson Professor of Manufacturing Management and a professor of operations, technology, and information management at Cornell's SC Johnson College of Business.

MAËLLE GAVET has worked in technology for 15 years. She served as Chief Operating Officer of Compass, Executive Vice President of operations at Priceline Group, and CEO of Ozon. She has been named a Young Global Leader by the World Economic Forum, one of *Fortune*'s 40 Under 40, and one of the Most Creative People in Business by *Fast Company*, and she was fifth on *Time* magazine's List of the Top 25 Female Techpreneurs. She is the author of *Trampled by Unicorns: Big Tech's Empathy Problem and How to Fix It* (2020).

ANNABELLE GAWER is a chaired professor in digital economy and Director of the Centre of Digital Economy at the University of Surrey, United Kingdom. She is a coauthor of *The Business of Platforms: Strategy in the Age of Digital Competition, Innovation, and Power* (2019).

SHOHINI GHOSE is a quantum physicist and professor of physics and computer science at Wilfrid Laurier University. She is the President of the Canadian Association of Physicists, a TED Senior Fellow, and the founding Director of the Laurier Centre for Women in Science.

ALEXANDRE GONFALONIERI is an AI consultant and project manager based in Paris/Basel. He was previously the Head of Innovation at DNA Global Analytics. He writes about AI and brain-computer interface. Follow him on Twitter @AGonfalonieri.

JULIA HAGEN is the Director of Regulatory and Politics at Germany's health innovation hub, where she advises the Federal Ministry of Health on the digital transformation of Germany's health-care system. Previously she led the digital health activities at Bitkom, Germany's digital association.

REGINA MARUCA is a senior editor with Accenture Research.

HENRIK MATTHIES is the Managing Director of Germany's health innovation hub, where he advises the Federal Ministry of Health on the digital transformation of Germany's health-care system. He is a serial entrepreneur and one of Europe's digital health pioneers.

JEANNE C. MEISTER is Managing Partner of the HR advisory and membership firm Future Workplace, coauthor of *The 2020 Workplace* (2010), and founder of the Future Workplace Academy.

SANJAY PODDER leads technology innovation for growth markets at Accenture.

MEHAK SARANG is a research associate at Harvard Business School and the Lunar Exploration Projects Lead for the MIT Space Exploration Initiative.

SHALABH KUMAR SINGH is a senior principal with Accenture Research.

ARIEL D. STERN is the Poronui Associate Professor of Business Administration at Harvard Business School, where she is a faculty affiliate of the Health Care Initiative and the Digital Initiative. She is a faculty member at the Harvard-MIT Center for Regulatory Science and Ariadne Labs and works with Germany's health innovation hub, advising the Federal Ministry of Health on the digital transformation of Germany's health-care system.

MATT WEINZIERL is the Joseph and Jacqueline Elbling Professor of Business Administration at Harvard Business

School and a research associate at the National Bureau of Economic Research. His research and teaching focus on the design of economic policy and the economics and business of space.

DAVID B. YOFFIE is the Max and Doris Starr Professor of International Business Administration at Harvard Business School. He is a coauthor of *The Business of Platforms: Strategy in the Age of Digital Competition, Innovation, and Power* (2019).

Index

academic approach, 6–7
accountability, 99–100,
  104–105
  racism and, 116–118
  self-regulation by social
  media and, 121–129
accounts payable management,
  50–51
advertising, 101, 102
AI. *See* artificial intelligence
  (AI)
airline reservation system,
  124–125
Alphabet, 98
Amazon, 4–5, 75, 98, 100
American Airlines, 124–125
Apple, 98, 100, 110, 122
application architectures, 138
Artemis Accords, 90
artificial intelligence (AI),
  xiv–xv
  academic approach to, 6–7
  biases in, xiv
  building ethical, 3–16
  energy use by, 132–133
  ethical deployment of, 14–15

explainability in, 12–13
  "on the ground" approach
  to, 7
  in health care, ethics and,
  10–12
  high-level approach to, 7–8
  risk framework and, 9–10
attention levels, monitoring, 63
audits, blockchain, 40–41,
  42, 51
Axiom Space, 86

Barton, LeRon L., xiv, 109–120
BCIs. *See* brain-computer
  interfaces (BCIs)
biases, xiv
  in AI, 4–5
  in the tech industry, 109–120
Big Bang Disruptions, xiii
bitcoin, 51–52, 54, 132
Blackman, Reid, xiv, 3–16
blockchain, xii, 35–57
  advantages of for supply
  chains, 37–41
  audits with, 40–41, 42

blockchain (*continued*)
consensus protocols, 54–55
definition of, 36
efficiency, speed, and disruptions with, 46–49
energy used by, 132
execution errors in, 38–40
financing, contracting, and international transactions with, 49–51
known participants in, 52–53
permissions in, 52–53
physical asset security and, 55–56
record keeping in, 41–43
smart contracts in, 43–44
traceability with, 44–46
transaction detail capture in, 38–39
workable technology for supply chains, 51–56
Blue Origin, 83
Boeing, 83
Bowman, Ronda, 23–24
brain-computer interfaces (BCIs), 61–70
applications of, 61–65
Brönneke, Jan B., 27–34
Brown, Robert H., 24
Bundesinstitut Für Arzneimittel und Medizinprodukte (BfArM, Germany), 28–29
Burden, Adam, 131–141
business models, 101–107

censorship, 121–122
change, speed of, xvi–xvii
cloud, energy use by the, 137–139
cognitive performance, 62
Cognizant, 22
Commercial Space Launch Competitiveness Act of 2015, 90
communication, quantum, 73–75
Communications Decency Act, Section 230, 122, 125, 126–127
confrontation, 114–115
conscious capitalism, 104–105
consensus protocols, 54–55
conspiracy theories, 121–122
containerization, 138
contracting, 43–44, 49–51
corporate social responsibility, 124
counterfeit goods, 46, 55–56
Covid-19 pandemic, xii, xv, 28, 32
cross-order trade, 50–51
cryptocurrencies, 36, 51–52, 54, 132
culture, AI ethics and, 13
customer service, 20–21
Cusumano, Michael A., xvii, 121–129

data centers, 137–139
data compression, 137–138
data ethics. *See also* artificial
    intelligence (AI)
  health care and, 30–32
  ownership of data and,
    67–68
  supply chains and, 47–48
Debatin, Jörg F., 27–34
Dede, Christopher, 18
DiGA registry, 29–30
Digitale-Versorgung-Gesetz
    (DVG, Germany), 27–34
Digital Healthcare Act (Ger-
    many), 27–34
direct-to-consumer (D2C)
    model, 103–104
disruption, xii–xiii
diversity, 109–120
double-spend problem, 48
Downes, Larry, xi–xviii
dystopian visions of the future,
    xiii–xiv

e-learning, 18–19
election, 2020 U.S. Presidential,
    100
Emerson, 36, 46–48
empathy, 20–21
employees
  evaluations, 23–24
  incentivizing for risk identifi-
    cation, 14

rights of, 103
  sustainability and, 134
  VR training for, 17–26
encryption, 73–75
enterprise-resource planning
    (ERP) systems, 37–41, 44
  environmental, social, and cor-
    porate governance, 133–134
ethics
  academic approach to, 6–7
  accountability and, 99–100
  AI and, 3–16
  brain-computer interfaces
    and, 66–68
  conscious capitalism and,
    100, 104–105
  in deployment, 14–15
  governance and, 8–9
  "on the ground" approach to, 7
  in health care, 10–12
  high-level AI principles on, 7–8
  incentivizing, 14
  operationalizing, 4–5, 7–15
  organizational awareness
    of, 13
  quantum computing and, 77
  risk framework and, 9–10
evaluations, employee, 23–24
explainability, 12–13

Facebook, 4, 98, 100, 101, 110
  U.S. Capitol insurrection and,
    121–122

fake news, 121–122
Fast-Track Process, 28–29
Federal Institute for Drugs and
    Medical Devices (Germany),
    28–29
financing, 49–51, 98–99
    diversity and, 110–111
flexibility, 134–135
functions-as-a-service (FaaS),
    138
Future Workplace, 19

Gaiha, Abhinav, 35–57
Gaur, Vishal, 35–57
Gavet, Maëlle, 97–108
Gawer, Annabelle, xvii,
    121–129
geopolitical rivalries, 91
Germany, digital health care
    apps in, 27–34
Ghose, Shonini, 71–79
Goldman Sachs, 3–4
Gonfalonieri, Alexandre, xiv,
    61–70
"good Samaritan" exception,
    126–127
Google, 75, 98, 110, 122,
    134
Google NLP, 22
governance, 8–9, 133–134
    blockchain and, 53
GSI standards, 41

Hagen, Julia, 27–34
Hatthies, Henrik, 27–34
Hayward, 36, 48
headbands, sensing, 62–63
health care
    acceptance of apps in, 30–31
    data protection in, 29–30
    digital tools in, 27–34
    ethics in, 10–12
    real-world data on, 31–32
HPE Financial Services
    (HPEFS), 23–24
H&R Block, 20–21

IBM, 3, 36, 45, 75
IBM Food Trust, 45
incentives for ethical behavior,
    14
infrastructure, 86
    AI ethics and, 8–9
innovation, xvii
Intel, 110, 136–137
international transactions,
    49–51
Internet of Things (IoT),
    46, 55
inventory, 37–41, 105. See also
    supply chains
    allocation decisions, 47–49
    security in, 55–56
    traceability of, 44–46
Iorns, Kim, 20–21

kanban systems, 48

leaders and leadership, xvii
    AI ethics and, 8–9, 14–15
    quantum computing and,
        76–77
    virtual reality for developing,
        17–26
lead times, 47–48
legal risks, 3–4

machine-learning algorithms,
        xiv
    explainability and, 12–13
Made In Space, Inc., 85–86
management, xiii
Maruca, Regina, 131–141
Meister, Jeanne C., xii,
        17–26
metrics, 135
microaggressions, 111
Microsoft, 75, 98, 100
movie industry rating system,
        124, 127

NASA, 83, 84, 85, 89
Nerurkar, Kshitij, 22
network effects, 122
neurofeedback training, 62
Nunes, Paul, xiii

onboarding, 21
organizational awareness, 13

ParallelDots API, 22
passthoughts, 66
performance, brain-computer
    interfaces and, 62–63
Pew Research, 100
pharmaceutical industry,
    44–45, 53, 54, 74
    quantum computing and,
        74–75
platform infrastructure
    businesses, 103–104
Podder, Sanjay, 131–141
presentation skills, 21–23
privacy issues, 66, 99
    advertising, 101, 102
probability, 72–73, 74. See also
    quantum computing
product managers, 12–13
professional events, 63–64
proof of work, 54
property rights, 89–90

quantum computing, 71–79
    classical physics vs., 72–73
    communication and, 73–75
    preparing for, 75–78
    quantum theory, 72–73
    qubits, 75–76

racism, 109–120
asking for help and, 116–118
being yourself and, 112–114
speaking up and, 114–115
randomized controlled trials,
31–32
real-world data, 31–32
regulation, xv–xvii
AI and, 3–4, 9
explainability of AI and, 13
of Germany's health care
apps, 27–34
self-, xvii, 121–129
of the space economy, 88–91
tech companies and, 99,
105–106
threats of, 123–124, 127–128
reputation, 3–4, 9
resilience, xiii
RFID tags, 41
risk, xiv–xvii
academic approach to, 6–7
AI and, 3–16
dominance of tech giants
and, 98
"on the ground" approach
to, 7
high-level AI principles on,
7–8
incentivizing identification
of, 14
operationalizing management
of, 7–15

organizational awareness
of, 13
planning for mitigation of,
5–6
space industries and, 88–91
round-robin protocol, 54–55

Sarang, Mehak, 81–93
science fiction, reality
approaching, xi–xviii
security issues, 66–68,
73–75, 76
server architectures, 138
serverless computing, 138
Sidewalk Labs, 5
Silicon Valley, 97–108
accountability of, 99–100
business models, 101–107
dominance of top companies
in, 98
financing and, 98–99
lack of diversity in, 109–120
legacy businesses and,
106–107
public trust in, 99–100
regulation and, 99, 105–106
self-regulation and, xviii,
121–129
taxes paid by, 100–101
simulations, 21–24
Singh, Shalabh Kumar, 131–141
smart contracts, 43–44

social media, self-regulation
by, 124–129
soft skills, xii, 17–26
software, 131–141
  development life cycle,
  135–137
  making the cloud green and,
  137–139
Software Development Assistant, 136–137
space industry, 81–93
  commercial, 83–88
  for creature comforts,
  86–88
  mining, 87–88
  moving beyond geopolitical
  rivalries in, 91
  regulation and support for,
  88–91
  research, 90
  space-for-earth economy, 82,
  83–84
  space-for-space economy,
  82–83, 84–85, 86, 88–91
SpaceX, 83, 84–85
stakeholders, 14–15, 134
Star Trek, xiii–xiv
Stern, Ariel D., 27–34
subscription models, 103–104
supply chains
  advantages of blockchain for,
  37–41
  audits, 40–41, 42

efficiency, speed, and disruptions in, 46–49
execution errors in, 38–40
financing, contracting, and
  international transactions,
  49–51
information, inventory, and
  financial flows in, 37–41
main function of, 36
physical asset security and,
  55–56
record keeping in, 41–43
reducing disruption in,
  46–49
smart contracts in, 43–44
traceability in, 44–46
transparency in, 35–57
workable blockchain
  technology for, 51–56
sustainability, 131–141

taxes, 100–101
technology
  blockchain, xii, 35–57
  brain-computer interfaces,
  61–70
  civilization defined by, xiv
  future of, 97–108
  optimism about, xi–xii
  quantum computing,
  71–79
  racism and, 109–120

technology (*continued*)
  self-regulation and, xvii,
    121–129
  software sustainability,
    131–141
  space industry, 81–93
  speed of change in, xvi–xvii
  trust in, xv, xvi, 99–100
telehealth, xii
tokenization, 55–56
trade-offs, 134–135
tragedy of the commons, 123,
    124
training, virtual reality for,
    17–26
transparency, supply chain,
    35–57
trust, xv, xvi
  blockchain and, 42, 52–53
  physical asset security and,
    55–56
  in technology, 99–100
"21 HR Jobs of the Future"
    (Meister and Brown), 24
Twitter, 110–111, 121–122

U.S. Capitol insurrection,
    121–122
U.S. Drug Supply Chain Secu-
    rity Act of 2013, 44–45
users, respecting, 11–12

utopian visions of the future,
    xiii–xiv

video game rating system, 124,
    127
Virgin Galactic, 83
virtual reality (VR), xii
  adoption rates for, 19
  benefits of, 18–19
  customer service training
    with, 20–21
  for employee evaluation,
    23–24
  immersion counselors, 24
  for presentation skills, 21–23
  for soft skills development,
    17–26
VR. *See* virtual reality (VR)

Walmart, 45
Walmart Canada, 49
Weinberger, David, xii
Weinzierl, Matt, 81–93
wellness programs, 63

Yoffie, David B., xvii, 121–129

"zero hours" contracts, 103

Is Your Business Ready for the Future?

ARTIFICIAL INTELLIGENCE

BLOCKCHAIN

CYBERSECURITY

If you enjoyed this book and want more on today's pressing business topics, turn to other books in the **Insights You Need** series from *Harvard Business Review*. Featuring HBR's latest thinking on topics critical to your company's success—from Blockchain and Cybersecurity to AI and Agile—each book will help you explore these trends and how they will impact you and your business in the future.